LIMITATIONS TO LIMITLESS

Seven Proven Strategies To Protect Your Finances From Life's Curveballs

Tanya Taylor, CPA, MBA

Award Winning Author & Speaker

TABLE OF CONTENTS

ACKNOWLEDGEMENTS

I would like to extend a very special thank you to my amazing daughters, Alana, and Jordyn who have had to make major adjustments over the past few years as I journeyed through my sudden disability. Thanks for your continued patience and unwavering support, and that little extra push when I need it. I am also deeply grateful to my family, medical providers, clients, friends, and members of the Grow Your Wealth Community.

INTRODUCTION

—An end is only defined by our agreement to halt progress; otherwise, we continue evolving from good to better, perpetually."

Imagine a bustling Saturday afternoon. You are behind the wheel, running errands with your daughter. Sunshine streams through the windows, casting a warm glow on the ordinary miracle of another beautiful summer day. Then, in a heartbeat, everything changes. A sudden jolt, followed by another, the screeching of tires and the sickening crunch of metal. The world you knew spins on its axis. Thankfully, the initial medical reports are reassuring—a minor car accident and a six-week disability leave. Relief washes over you. You have always been a planner, someone who prioritizes security. You have disability insurance and an emergency fund; you should be okay.

Except, you are not. A cruel twist of fate—a seemingly insignificant change in your employer's disability policy—throws your carefully constructed financial safety net into disarray. A slight panic claws its way up your throat. This was not supposed to happen. You were prepared! Were you not?

What Does This Book Have For You?

The truth is many of us fall into the same trap. We never think about becoming disabled or think that we are prepared if something of the sort happens. However, this only leads us to discovering the devastating financial consequences of disability. Statistics paint a sobering picture: According to Social Security data, one in four working-age Americans over the age of twenty will experience a disability before retiring. Even more alarming, various studies have shown that a significant portion of bankruptcy filings stem directly from loss of income due to medical issues, plunging families into financial despair.

This book is for you - the healthy skeptic who believes disability is a distant worry, the individual already facing the challenges of living with a disability, and most importantly, those who, like me, strive for financial security.

My Purpose For This Book

Imagine building your dream life, brick by brick, financially. That is the promise of my book, *"Broke to Wealth."* But while I was writing, it hit me: what if something unexpected derailed your plans? Like it did for me! What steps do people need to take now to prepare?

Talking to countless individuals, I realized a scary truth: most people had no idea how they would handle a disability. Financially, it could be devastating. I wrote this book to share practical steps that you can take to mitigate the impact and strategies to ensure you keep your disability benefits.

Disability is not a topic that most people think about, and why should they? It is dull; it is a drag, and quite frankly, who wants to think about becoming disabled? No one.

Now I get that many people have strong opinions about insurance and why it's one of the biggest legal scams. I like to call it a necessary evil. It has always been one of my key risk management tools, and when I work with clients, we always discuss how vitally important it is to carve out money in their budget to purchase insurance.

I had been a big advocate of insurance before I ever worked in the insurance industry, and despite knowing what I do about the industry, I continue to be an advocate for all types of insurance. To be clear, I have never sold insurance policies, and therefore have no vested interest in anyone purchasing a policy. I do however believe that each policy has its place. Insurance can serve as wonderful risk management and wealth building tools, but it is important that each of us evaluate which policies are best suited for our families.

We purchase homeowners' insurance, even if our home is fully paid for, because most of us cannot replace our home in cash if it gets destroyed. Think about disability insurance in that same way. Disability insurance is a type of insurance that replaces some or all of your income when you become disabled from an illness or injury and cannot work. Since most of us will struggle if we have a significant reduction in our income long term, think of this insurance as the gap between what you earn now and what you will need to survive. I purchased a long-term disability policy years ago, to supplement my employer's policy which only covered 60% of my income.

When I had the car accident, I did not feel panicked after learning a few days later that I would be out on disability for about 6 weeks. I knew I would be fine because of my disability insurance through my job and my emergency fund.

What I had not realized was that my employer had changed the terms of their short-term disability policy less than a year earlier, so they now had a look-back period. These things can get a bit tricky so allow me to simplify. Essentially, what that means is that if I used my short-term disability insurance in the past year, I would only be covered for the amounts that I did not use. Just my luck, I had used up most of my short-term disability insurance and only had two weeks of benefits left.

There are many nuances to disability insurance. It can be quite complex, but it is necessary for each of us to have a baseline knowledge. Ideally, you want to have this knowledge before you suffer a disabling event. So, if you are reading this while you are healthy, this is perfect. Now is the best time, because you will be able to prepare yourself in case you become an unlucky victim of an unexpected, disabling event.

If you are thinking that you will not become disabled, you are in good company—most of us think the same thing. But statistics show otherwise—one in four is a very significant number. My hope for you is that you never suffer a disabling event. However, life is filled with uncertainties. I want to share with you everything that I have learned, so if you become disabled you can have not just the knowledge, but also a good foundation established.

If you have already experienced a disabling condition, you will still find invaluable information throughout the chapters of this book. Let us create a movement by sharing this book with our friends and families so that they can become educated and protected without having to worry about filing for bankruptcy.

Disclaimer: I am not an attorney. This book is written based on my experience living with a sudden disability and going through the long-term disability process. Throughout the book, I will make recommendations about consulting your human resource office and disability attorneys, since they can best interpret and provide guidance about the language in the contracts. My role here is to share with you the practical day-to-day nuances and how the terms of a contract can be implemented, while simplifying technical insurance jargons and blending what I do best—providing financial guidance on how to navigate the world of unexpected disability without losing it all.

What You Will Learn

By the end of this journey, you will have gained a practical knowledge base using the following seven strategies outlined in this book:

- **Build a Financial Safety Net**

  - **Budget for success:** We will discuss the importance of creating a realistic budget, prioritizing essential expenses, and exploring cost-cutting strategies to ensure we live comfortably within our new income bracket.

- **Understand the Complexities of Short-Term & Long-Term Disability**

  - Demystify the qualifications needed to receive benefits, and learn about the typical length of coverage, changes in total income, how long we need to wait to receive benefits and how short-term disability interplays with long term disability benefits.

- **Learn how to shop for a policy**

  - You will learn how to determine whether you have the right amount of coverage, and what to do if you don't, and how to shop for a policy that is suitable for you.

- **How to secure and keep your benefits**

  - Learn to effectively communicate your medical situation, gather crucial medical records, and navigate the appeals process if our claim is denied.

- **Fight for your benefits and avoid pitfalls**

  - Learn from my many challenges and areas where I got blindsided, so you do not repeat them, and understand how to secure the experts to help you get what you rightfully deserve.

- **Social Security Disability Income (SSDI) as a lifeline**

  - Understand the role SSDI plays in disability, the process for applying and how it differs from Social Security Income (SSI) and Unemployment.

- **Building resilience and looking forward:**

  - Disability is not a death sentence, and we can live a fulfilling life, even if we do not return to the lives we previously led. While we acknowledge the challenges of the emotional and social impact, we discuss some practical ways to stop the fear and feel empowered to protect our future.

We cannot predict the future, but we can prepare. Let us turn "prepared" into "peace of mind." Let's start building our safety nets today and not wait for a crisis to take us down!

CHAPTER 1

Great Was The Fall

—It's good to plan for the unexpected, even if it doesn't work out as you think it will."

Let's go back to 1988, when I first left my homeland: Jamaica. Growing up I faced extreme poverty. This is what drove me to seek financial security. After graduating from high school at 16, I received an opportunity to move to the United States. With $100 in my pocket, a visa that was expiring in a month, and no idea where I would live permanently, I set off to the land of opportunity: America. A country that we had heard so much about—it was described in such magical ways that we would imagine streets paved with gold, where we could achieve anything.

The moment I stepped off the flight, I pictured a swift climb out of this rut. A good job, a return to school—a clear path forward. That, however, was not my reality. For years, I shared a room with three young boys, living paycheck to paycheck, with poverty still snaking its serpentine head around every corner, and in the lives of everyone around me.

Despite the obstacles, I was undaunted. I had big dreams, and I was going to make my dreams a reality. I began by studying successful people, learning everything I could about them, and setting out to emulate them. My vision was not to just stop the cycle of poverty in my family, but to build wealth.

I created a list of goals and began to check them off one by one. Some notable achievements were:

- Graduating from college debt-free at 25 with a plethora of job offers. As I grew in my profession, my work would allow me to touch most of the largest banks and insurance companies globally.

- I ventured into entrepreneurship by becoming co-owner of a small business at age 24, and a few years later I started a tax practice with my husband.

- Purchased an income-producing home 6 months before college graduation. While I had tremendous struggles with this home over many years, it has been a wonderful investment that will benefit me for years to come.

- Co-founding a stock market investment club with my friends, making smart investments that allowed me to build my retirement to seven figures before age 48 while simultaneously funding my children's college education.

- Hitting 50 countries before 50, because I truly believe that we need to enjoy the journey of life and not wait until some magical age to start doing the things that we love, all with little or no consumer debt.

For twenty-four years, I climbed the corporate ladder, meticulously ticking goals off a list I had compiled in my ambitious youth. Now, the ultimate goal loomed: starting my own business and severing ties with the corporate world.

While working on that plan, my dream job came calling. But fate, it seemed, had a different plan. One unforeseen event would send everything I had built tumbling down. The million-dollar question was: **Were my guardrails solid enough to hold me up?**

I DID NOT SEE THIS COMING

Security blanket—that is what my friends called it. It's when every kind of insurance relevant for your life is neatly tucked into your portfolio. The emergency fund was also checked off. Usually, double the recommended amount. Yes, I got teased for my obsession with a "high need for security," but I craved stability, and truthfully, I feared ever going back to where I started.

Life, no matter how meticulously planned, throws curveballs. That is the whole point of "unexpected," after all. You never know what is around the corner or when it will hit.

So, there I was, brimming with grand ambitions. It was the thick of the COVID pandemic, and I had just soft launched my new business, eager to take it to the next level. Receiving the call for my dream job presented a bit of trepidation. When I was at this crossroads, I had three different options:

1. I had completed the five years I had given myself at my job. There were lots of changes taking place in my department, and I was bored to tears. I would also need to disclose my business at some point, and I wasn't sure whether it would be viewed as a conflict of interest. So, overall, it just felt like the right time to jump ship.

2. I had set a goal about 6 years ago to leave corporate by September 1, 2021. I was behind due to COVID, but do I walk away and immerse myself fully in my business, using the cushion I had built up to carry me through? Or lastly,

3. Do I check off the last goal on my journey through corporate America? This was the position that I always told myself that I wanted to end my corporate career with.

Ultimately, I decided to interview for the role and then decide after the offer. I figured that I had never applied for a job and had not succeeded in landing the position, so the odds were in my favor. I rationalized that I could take the job, spend the next two years ensuring the foundations of my business were solid, and then move on to my next chapter.

The first round of interviews for Senior Vice President and Head of Accounting Policy at one of the world's largest independent investment banks, went exceedingly well.

With an emergency fund covering almost one year of expenses, and other passive income, I felt that I was in a relatively good place financially. Having risk assessed my expenses, I believed I could weather any financial storm. But I didn't know that the one that was about to hit would test everything.

It was a beautiful Saturday morning in August 2021. My day was booked solid. At about 11:30 a.m., my entire life was upended—physically and financially.

I was finalizing repairs for my move and preparing for the second round of interviews. I had just left the house to take my daughter on a quick errand when, BOOM! We were violently rear-ended.

In total shock, I tried to pull off to the side, but in the process, we felt a much bigger impact! This launched everything, including the center console in our car, in different directions and left us screaming in terror. My head violently swung forward, then backward, slamming against the back of the headrest. Other than an immediate headache, I felt fine physically but in terror emotionally.

As I looked around to see what had hit us, a figure approached. Was this the Grim Reaper coming to collect his due? If so, where was his scythe?

It was a young man in his early twenties walking slowly toward us like a zombie. I worried he was coming to get his revenge on us for the damage to his car. We all know how people love their cars in America.

Our life is over, I thought, and I panicked. I could see that same fear in my daughter's eye as I checked to see how I could quickly plot her escape. She was frozen, just as I was.

The good news was that he was not a killer. He came over to apologize. He had suffered a medical emergency, and was in a state of shock as well.

I was able to breathe and call my hubby, who insisted the EMT treat all of us. I told him, *"I do not have time for hospitals; I have a job interview to prepare for and a house to move into before our guests arrive on Monday!"*

When the driver's family members arrived and asked if I was okay, I said, *"No, I am not okay."* I held up and pointed to an entry in my detailed daily planner and screamed, *"You see! Car accidents and near-death experiences were NOT part of my schedule today."* Just kidding. I didn't do that. But in my head, that's what I was pointing to. And I certainly did not have time to start crying, but that is what I did.

The next day, I still felt fine—I thought, brilliant! I will just get back in the swing of things. But the day after that, I could not get out of bed. My entire right side was sore, weak, numb, and tingling. I could not turn my neck to the right and could barely raise my arm. I had several herniated and bulging discs in my upper and lower spine, and a torn rotator cuff.

Initially, the doctors told me that I should do therapy for six weeks, then they would assess how I was feeling and see if I would need more extensive therapy. My response, as you might guess, was a resounding, *"I do not have time for therapy!"* This was also when I was actively planning how to check off my bucket list item of 50 countries before 50, so slowing down and going to therapy 3 times a week was not a part of any of my plans.

As it turns out, it did not matter what plans I had; the next few years would be some of the most difficult years of my life. There were a total of three surgeries, plus steroid injections recommended.

When you have an accident and you are on disability, there is pressure for you to have surgery, even when you are being told that the surgery may not provide incremental relief. I will discuss this in more detail later. My injuries created many different limitations, which impacted my ability to work.

So, begrudgingly, I had to give up on working in any job. I had put so much energy and resources into creating my business, so I pushed and pushed, but eventually I had to put it on pause, and take the time to focus on my health. During that period, one of my daughters was also going through the worst time of her young life, health-wise, which also required a lot of my time and attention.

For almost three years, chronic pain has been a relentless companion. It opened the door for unwelcome guests—depression and anxiety—who had settled in and made themselves comfortable. Exacerbated by the fact that I was now dependent solely on entities that could yank my income away at their discretion while I was unable to physically work. All made for terrible roommates.

This accident was not just a career setback; it was a full-on life pause. The dream of generational wealth for myself and my family suddenly felt precariously balanced on a tightrope. We will unpack the specifics throughout the book.

As someone who thrived on meticulously planning every detail, this experience was a brutal lesson in the power of the unexpected. The financial burden of my disability, coupled with large, unexpected expenses and a reduction in income, has been a very heavy weight to carry.

I am sharing all the details that I can, because I think it is important that you understand how quickly your life could change and your financial security become threatened. Living through this disability has taught me so much about priorities, and financial security, but even more about finding that balance that allows me to relinquish some of my fear and rigidity, while continuing to plan responsibly.

IS THERE SUCH A THING AS A PERFECTLY PLANNED LIFE?

I don't believe life can be perfectly planned, but what if we can plan for possible real-life events that could have a significant financial impact. Even in doing so, we may not hit a home run, but perhaps we will touch most of the bases. I have always had a risk-management process in place, where I test different scenarios that could have a significant impact on my income.

"What if X happens?" I would ask myself, then map out worst-case outcomes and contingency plans. I am happy that I did those exercises. But with that said, when life throws a curveball—especially a long-term one, followed by several others, the reality check can be brutal. What that planning does, however, is give you a solid foundation, so that even when the bricks start falling, you don't completely crash and burn.

Here is how the scenarios played out financially after the accident:

During August 2021, when the accident happened, I had been on and off Short-term disability for about nine months and used up all but two weeks of my Short-term disability benefits. My employer's long-term disability plan would not start for another six months. The supplemental policy I purchased, which was close to forty percent of my salary, would kick in in three months.

So, what did that mean? It meant that I had only two weeks of income from my job, and then I would have no other income for almost three months until I began receiving my private disability income. I would then have to wait an additional three months for the income from the policy that my job offered to kick in. My plan was to use my emergency fund as well as some of my other resources.

How the income piece worked

If I made $10,000 monthly, this is what it looked like.

- For 2 weeks, I would receive my full salary.
- For the next—almost—3 months, I would need to pull $10,000 out of my emergency fund each month for a total of $30,000.
- From month 3 to 6, I would need to take out $6,000 from my emergency fund each month, since my private disability policy that covers close to 40% of my income would kick in - $18,000 total emergency fund withdrawal.
- So, for six months, just to maintain my monthly expenses without considering any unexpected costs, I would need to pull a total of $48,000 from my emergency fund.

Here was my reality during that time:

- I had a renovation project with large overruns. Some of these overruns were financed by my emergency fund.

- I had a tenant that I needed to get out of my house. I knew that once I gave her notice, she would take advantage of New York's draconian landlord-tenant laws and stop paying her rent, which means she could live in my home rent-free for upward of two years or even longer while we go through the court system. A significant decrease in my passive income stream.

- I could no longer cook, so UberEATS became a close family friend. My children also ended up relying on Uber more often because of my driving challenges.

- Physical therapy using the no-fault insurance coverage from the auto insurer provided very little relief, so I hired my own physical therapist which cost a few hundred dollars each month.

- My largest, unexpected expense of all was my daughter's illness. Most of her medical costs were not covered by insurance, and some months costs were in the thousands.

- I had invested heavily in my coaching business and felt challenged in making big decisions about it. If I continued to pursue my business, I could potentially receive no disability income. I was fine with that aspect because I knew that if I could do my business in a sustainable way, I would be able to replace my income. The optimist in me was ready to go, so I pushed myself for a while and gave it my all. Over time, however, reality set in. Pushing through pain daily while managing clients and the administrative aspects of a new business showed me a humbling reality. I could not show up the way I needed to. Reluctantly, I decided to put my business on pause. This was one of my rock bottom moments.

  To avoid having to start all over again, there were some fixed expenses, such as website and system costs, and the salary of a virtual assistant that I continued to incur.

Do you see how quickly life went from the status quo to falling apart effortlessly? Even with careful planning, an unexpected, disabling event can easily send you spiraling financially. If I did not have an emergency fund and other resources in place, I would have found myself in a serious financial crisis.

Very Important Note: Don't expect that your insurance will begin paying immediately on the date it goes into effect. I did not receive the first check from my private policy until March (instead of December), and the one from my job started in May instead of February. You will need to be prepared for those delays and plan financially. If you are wondering about Social Security disability income, I have dedicated an entire section to it. **Knowing how to prepare for the unexpected can be the difference between surviving and thriving.**

KEY TAKEAWAYS

- **The unexpected can derail even the most meticulously planned life.** I had a strong financial foundation and clear goals, but a car accident forced me to hit pause on my dreams.

- **Financial preparedness is crucial.** Disability insurance and an emergency fund can help us weather unexpected financial hardship.

- **Disability can be emotionally challenging.** Denial, anxiety, and depression are common responses to a disabling event.

- **Be prepared to adjust your plans.** In addition to giving up my job, I had to put my business dreams on hold to focus on my health.

- **There is no such thing as a perfectly planned life.** Life throws curveballs, so be prepared to adapt and overcome challenges.

Buckle up! This chapter serves as a wake-up call, highlighting the unexpected turns that life can take. But fear not! Having emerged from this experience with a new and deeper understanding, I am eager to share the valuable lessons I learned. Now, we will tackle the first reality that hits you after a disabling event: adjusting your finances to the current situation to secure your future.

CHAPTER 2

Safeguard Your Future: **Budgeting and Adjustments**

—Focusing on the details of our financial flow creates security; it does not signal trouble, but good stewardship"

Listen, you may not like what you are about to hear, but this is necessary. It is one of the things that people fight against repeatedly, but no matter how much we fight against it, we have no choice but to face it. So, let's take the pressure off and move forward together without resistance.

Let's talk about budgeting, or as you can call it, a spending plan. In general, everyone needs some kind of guide that tells them how much money they have coming in and how much of it is going out. Without that guide, we may end up in debt with little to no savings. Believe it or not, most of us have no idea how we spend our money, and we have no idea when we will pay off the debt we have accumulated.

One of the first things I generally do with my clients, and something I have done since I was 16, is to create a budget. You do not need a fancy spreadsheet. You can use an app — visit my website at growyourwealth10x.com for a free, ready-to-print download that lists different apps you can use, as well as a free budget template. Ultimately, you should know how much money is coming in and how much is going out.

When you suffer a disabling event, your expenses may shift quite significantly, depending on the type of disability you have. Here is an example of what I mean by that.

Before the accident, I did not dine out much and mostly prepared my meals at home. I also did my hair myself and drove my children to their activities. After I became disabled, I was unable to do these things. As mentioned earlier, my Uber bill skyrocketed for food and transportation, and I had to start paying to get my hair done because I could not do it on my own.

Having family and friends to assist us may be helpful, but once this becomes long-term, ongoing assistance can be less realistic because everyone has their own lives to lead.

With this understanding, we will realize the importance of knowing what we have coming in and what we are spending, so that we can maintain control of our finances and avoid going deep into financial struggles. If you are already in the habit of budgeting, you are way ahead of the game and will just need to adjust it based on your new circumstances. If you have no budget, jumpstart the process now. With a budget, you can identify ways to align spending habits with goals and build a financial cushion.

It is important that our budget is realistic. If it is not, we will find ourselves in a constant financial battle until we give up. For example, if coffee expenses are $7 daily and no changes are expected, no adjustments should be made for that line item. Let's not try to make it aspirational by only budgeting $20 weekly. Instead, find something else to cut back on and include the full cost of the coffee in your budget. Otherwise, you are setting yourself up for disappointment and pushing yourself deeper into debt.

In my book *"Broke to Wealth"*, now available on Amazon.com or at growyourwealth10x.com, I have detailed very effective strategies for tracking your expenses and creating an optimized spending plan or budget. But that's not all. I've also differentiated between the two to help you determine which is best for you.

After learning how to track your spending and creating a budget/spending plan, you will be able to filter out some unnecessary expenses and channel all that extra money to your emergency fund.

As someone with a disabling condition, you may spend more than the average person on your medical and living expenses and incur additional types of expenses. For this reason, an emergency fund is vital to cover any unexpected expenses.

Having a budget is the foundation for helping you create an emergency fund, because you will know what your true monthly expenses are. If there is a lapse between when you stop receiving your income and when your disability income begins, or if your disability income does not replace your salary, your emergency fund will help to fill the gap. It may mean that your entire emergency fund will be wiped out.

In my case, although I had almost a year's worth of savings set aside, mine was all but gone by the time I started receiving my disability income. Those one-time and other large, unexpected expenses were brutal! The idea is that once you begin receiving income, or if you receive any lump-sum money, you begin to rebuild. You should have an emergency fund before, during, and after a disability.

HEALTHCARE COST CONSIDERATIONS

- **Health Insurance Premiums:** Since disability will impact your ability to work, you must consider how you will be able to maintain employer-sponsored health insurance or if you will need to seek COBRA or alternative health insurance plans, which may be at a higher cost than you are currently paying.

- **Increased Out-of-Pocket Costs:** Your disability might require additional medical treatment, medications, or therapies, leading to higher out-of-pocket healthcare costs that you will need to budget for.

- **Government-provided health insurance:** Research to see whether you qualify for any Medicaid or other government supplemented insurance programs.

STRATEGIES FOR MANAGING THE GAP

Having a readily available emergency fund can help bridge the income gap during the waiting period, but you will also need to:

- **Review your expenses:** Evaluate your current expenses and identify areas to cut back.

- **Check out government programs:** Explore government assistance programs you might qualify for, such as social security disability income (SSDI) or SSI.

- **SNAP Benefits:** Depending on your income and assets, you may qualify for the Supplemental Nutrition Assistance Program.

DISABLED WITH NO EMERGENCY FUND?

During Covid a statistic that was quoted frequently was that many Americans cannot afford an emergency expense over $400. If you are able-bodied, now is a good time to get started building your budget so that you can create or increase your emergency fund. I will also discuss ways to cut expenses later in the chapter. First things first, you need to properly analyze your expenses.

ANALYZING YOUR EXPENSES: BEFORE AND AFTER DISABILITY

When you have a change in your income, you must go back to the drawing board with a new eye to see how you will manage when you have less money coming in. Here are some things to look at:

- **Basic Living Expenses:** These include housing costs, utilities, groceries, and transportation. Evaluate if these expenses can be trimmed or if you can negotiate with your creditor. Also, investigate any benefits that you might now be eligible for.

- **New Expenses Due to Disability:** Depending on your situation, new costs might arise. In such cases you need to consider:

  - **Transportation:** If you cannot drive, rideshare services like Uber or Lyft might become necessary. Some of this may be offset by your transportation costs for work, but it's not always a one-for-one.

  - **Personal Care:** If you need assistance with daily activities, you might need to hire help. The reality is that our families and friends may not always be there long-term.

  - **Medical Equipment:** Certain disabilities might require specialized equipment that is not covered by insurance, adding to your expenses.

  - **Additional Cost:** You may need to hire someone to care for your young child—someone to do your laundry, cooking, cleaning, and other everyday tasks that you can no longer do.

Be prepared for those realities by evaluating where your needs will be and how they will be accomplished.

This analysis will expose areas where you can potentially cut back and those areas where you will increase your budget.

WHAT IF I CANNOT SAVE ENOUGH FOR AN EMERGENCY FUND?

For many people, the idea of hearing the word *"emergency fund"* brings a lot of anxiety. They think, "*Well, right now I am actually spending more than I am earning, so how is it possible that I could find extra cash to build an emergency fund?"*

For clarity, an emergency fund is a savings account that you can use to cover unexpected expenses, such as medical bills, car repairs, or loss of income. Put simply, it is money you have set aside that you will need access to in case something unexpected happens—that could mean suddenly becoming disabled. If you haven't quite figured out how emergency funds work, then worry not because in my book *"Broke to Wealth"*, I've dedicated an entire chapter to that.

Having an emergency fund can help you avoid getting into unwanted debt. It will reduce your stress and increase your financial security simultaneously.

You will also often hear the term, sinking fund. The key difference between an emergency fund and a sinking fund is what you are planning for. An emergency fund is for the unplanned, while a sinking fund is for predictable, planned expenses.

Here is a table to illustrate the difference:

Features	Emergency Fund	Sinking Fund
Purpose	Unexpected expenses	Planned expenses
Examples	Medical bills, Car repairs	Change roof, holiday gifts
Amount	3-6 months of living expenses	Varies depending on goals
Time Frame	Ongoing	Know, usually short to medium term

Let's say your car suddenly stops working due to issues with the transmission, and it costs $5,000 to repair it. If you have a healthy emergency fund, you can pay for it without going into debt. If you knew beforehand that after eighty thousand miles you would need to change your transmission, then you could have created a sinking fund for the $5,000. In this case, you would not need to touch your emergency fund. You can have many different sinking funds.

It is generally recommended that you have three to six months of income in your emergency fund. While I do not want to scare you, my situation should highlight to you that three to six months may not be enough. This might all sound daunting, especially if you don't know where to begin. So, if you are someone who struggles with your finances, here are five examples of quick ways you can find some cash for your emergency fund.

1. **Limit Ridesharing & Takeout Services:** Using Uber or UberEATS frequently can strain your budget. Explore more cost-effective alternatives like public transportation and cooking at home.

2. **Avoid bank fees:** Switch to a free checking and savings account with no minimum balance requirements. Keep a buffer in your checking account to avoid overdraft fees or consider an overdraft line of credit. Skip using other banks' ATMs to avoid high fees. Doing this alone can help you save quite a bit.

3. **Fight Parking Tickets and Fines:** Always ensure that you have put enough time on the meter to avoid parking tickets. Consider parking garages with flat fees instead and use parking apps. Keep your car registration and inspection updated and stay within city speeding limits to minimize fines.

4. **Shop with a Grocery List:** For many of us, we can go to our cupboards and refrigerators and see many items that expire unused. Many of these are impulse purchases. This is something that you need to avoid by sticking to a grocery list. Consider using apps like *"Our Groceries"* to keep track of family needs and streamline shopping trips.

5. **Monetize your passion:** What is something that you are good at? Identify ways that you can make money doing it and generate additional income.

When you reduce your spending by any combination of these items or others that you identify, you will unlock hidden savings in your budget! This newfound cash can fuel your emergency fund. If you have already suffered a disabling event, your list may look different, depending on your disability. For example, if you had a car that you drove for work only, do you still need that car? You could save on car payments, insurance, and gas.

DO YOU NEED TO DOWNSIZE?

You could find yourself in varying scenarios. For example, you have become disabled and do not have an emergency fund, but you are getting short-term or long-term disability income. You are self-employed and do not have a disability policy; or your short-term disability is less than 100% of your income. **What should you do?**

To stay afloat, you will need to start making some very tough decisions. The question about downsizing might not be one that you ask yourself immediately after you become disabled, but ultimately, you may need to consider it based on your financial circumstances.

You will need to start reflecting early on about your current lifestyle—your current expenses, what future expenses will look like, whether you can live the same lifestyle you want to live, or even how you will manage financially right now.

If you do not believe you can fund your current lifestyle, then you must start looking at how you will downsize. Downsizing does not necessarily mean you have to sell your home. That's a common misconception that most people have. In reality, selling your home and trying to purchase a smaller one may not be the most feasible solution. Depending on where you live, you may still not be able to afford a new home.

Downsizing may mean that if you live in a house with three floors, you rent out one of the floors, even if it is temporary, until you get back on your feet. It may mean getting a different car than the one you currently drive, or it may mean dining out less.

At the end of the day, you want to live comfortably and focus on your healing, not be stressed over the decisions you could have made. Nor do you want to compromise yourself so much that now you are trying to manage your illness while being miserable. Finding a balance will be key.

DO YOU HAVE A LOT OF DEBT?

Many of us struggle with debt, but it's important to understand that this struggle results from limited knowledge, and often, limiting beliefs. During a disability, that debt does not go away. The mere thought of looking at credit card statements and bills can trigger fear, shame, and regret, leading to a tendency to ignore the problem.

We can identify ways to reduce debt by utilizing different debt reduction strategies. Two popular methods are the snowball method and the avalanche method.

- **The snowball method** involves tackling your smallest debt first. Once it is paid off, the money from that debt is applied to the next smallest debt. You continue making minimum payments on all other debts, minimizing the impact on your credit score. As you pay off each debt, you gain a sense of accomplishment, which can be psychologically motivating. However, this method can prove to be more expensive in the long run.

- **The avalanche method** prioritizes debts based on interest rates. The debt with the highest interest rate is repaid first, while you make minimum payments on all others. Since you are tackling the highest interest rate first, you ultimately pay less interest overall compared to the snowball method. This method might be less motivating initially because it takes longer to see individual debts disappear.

Now, one of the most common questions here is how one can choose the right method and the answer to that greatly depends on the type of person you are. The snowball method can be ideal for you if you benefit from quick wins and a sense of progress. The avalanche method might be better for those of you who are more disciplined and prioritize saving money on interest. So, you will need to weigh the pros and cons of each method to decide which one aligns better with your situation.

I go into details about how to pay down your debt in my book, *"Broke to Wealth: How to Build a Strong Financial Foundation, Implement Effective Strategies, and Sustain Financial Growth,"* which you can find on Amazon.com or at growyourwealth10x.com.

KEY TAKEAWAYS

- Budgeting is essential for everyone, but especially for us with disabilities, as expenses can shift significantly.

- You need to create a realistic budget that tracks your income and expenses.

- Having an emergency fund is crucial to cover unexpected costs that may arise due to a disability.

- Analyze your expenses to see where you can cut back and free up money to save.

- There are ways to find hidden savings in your budget, such as limiting takeout and rideshare services.

- Downsizing your lifestyle may be necessary, depending on your financial situation.

- There are debt reduction strategies, such as the snowball and avalanche methods, to help manage debt.

Now that you have graduated to financial defense against disability's surprise attacks—budgeting and emergency funds conquered—let us unlock the secret weapon many have, but few understand: Short- and long-term disability insurance. The next chapter cracks the code on disability insurance, introducing you to the basics: the different types of benefits, the easiest way to calculate your benefit and payout percentages, and much more. See you there!

CHAPTER 3

The Power of Preparedness: **Do you have enough disability benefits?**

—Learning every aspect of a major life transition prevents exploitation of ignorance; life improves when we know how to make it better."

Have you ever gotten a medical diagnosis that felt like a bad punchline to a terrible joke? The kind that leaves you staring at the doctor, mouth agape, wondering if there is a hidden camera crew about to burst in and reveal it is all just a prank?

That is how being told that my injuries were life-altering and that it could take years for me to recover felt for me. One minute I was *"the queen of killing it,"* interviewing for my dream job, building my business, and planning my bucket list to hit 50 countries before 50. The next? The routine of using ice packs and taking painkillers to numb the pain replaced the constant hustle and bustle of life and shrunk my world. This was by no means the life I had imagined living. Gone were the days of hours of conference calls, running nine to twelve miles a day, and finding the craziest adventures while on vacation. Instead, my calendar was filled with specialist appointments and consultations, a brutal reminder of the new reality I had to face and how fast life can change.

Here is the thing about being told that you've had a life-altering event: while it stirs up a lot of emotions, you mainly go into denial. Denial is the first of the five stages of grief. You may think the doctors are wrong and that this is temporary. You rationalize — I will get back to what I used to do in no time.

I went through the three other stages—anger, bargaining, and depression. Truth be told, I don't know when I will get to fully accept everything; but I am working on a balance.

I was already aware of what long and short-term disability was, and I had bought my own personal long-term disability years ago. It is a different ball game experiencing a disabling event than merely preparing for it.

This chapter is all about untangling the mysteries of long-term disability and its sidekick, short-term disability, often referred to as LTD and STD. We will break down the differences, explore the types of benefits available, and shed some light on this often-confusing corner of the insurance world. Consider it your roadmap to maneuvering this unexpected detour, because knowledge is power, especially when it comes to protecting your financial well-being.

UNDERSTANDING DISABILITY AND OTHER TYPES OF BENEFITS

The Two Sides of the Coin: Short-Term vs. Long-Term Disability

The disability diagnosis was a gut punch for me. A screeching halt to the fast-paced world in which I thrived. The truth is, despite what the doctor said, I was sure it would be short-lived, so even when my Human Resources office began explaining my long-term disability benefits. I did not pay attention. I was chasing something greater when all of this happened, and I was moving full force ahead. I wasn't after those benefits and didn't need to know the details of this policy, because I would never get to that stage where I needed to activate my benefits because I was certain I would be back to working full-time long before that.

Let me tell you this: **Now is the time to pay attention**—before you have a disabling event. Here is where the two sides of the coin come in.

Disability Insurance benefits are benefits that replace your income if you cannot work due to an illness or an accident. It is not mandated by law in all states, therefore not all employers offer these benefits.

For employees who do not receive these benefits as part of their employer's benefits package, you and self-employed individuals will need to purchase your own policy.

SHORT-TERM DISABILITY (STD) BENEFITS

STD benefits are offered to cover your salary for temporary illnesses, such as having surgery or giving birth and staying home for a while. These benefits generally last six months, but in this changing world of employee benefits, it is wise to check with your employer to verify how long your benefit lasts and what percentage of your income you will receive. Better safe than sorry, right? What I mean is that just because you may receive payments for 6 months (26 weeks), it does not mean you will receive the full amount of your salary.

Each company has its own variations, so you must understand what your company offers. For example, your short-term disability benefits package may be structured so that you receive a full salary for the first 12 weeks and then 80% of your salary for the remaining 14 weeks if you have been with the company for less than 5 years. But if you have been with the company for a few decades, you may receive the entire 26 weeks of your salary in full. These variations are quite common. While you can purchase a short-term disability policy on your own, it is costly. Policies may also have additional eligibility requirements – for example you must be full time, or you must have worked with the company for at least one year.

Many policies have a *"look-back provision"* where the company will not pay STD income for more than six months in a twelve-month period, even if you become disabled for a different condition. This means that if you have used up the full amount of your disability income in less than twelve months and you become ill again in that twelve-month period, you will not receive any short-term disability income.

My situation was a perfect example of that. At the time of the accident, I had used up all but 2 weeks of my short-term disability benefits in a nine-month period. During those nine months, there were times when I was out of work 100% of the time, and at other times I worked a few days per week. As luck would have it, that same year, my company changed the policy to add the look-back provisions. Because I had already taken twenty-four weeks, the only short-term disability income that I was entitled to was two weeks, leaving me to fill the gap with my emergency funds and other resources. Are you beginning to see how essential these funds are?

LONG-TERM DISABILITY (LTD)

LTD insurance is a benefit that is provided to you either by your employer or that you can purchase on your own. It is intended to replace a portion of your income if you become disabled for an extended period. Depending on the policy, you could be covered through to age 65, when you become eligible for Social Security benefits.

Policies offered by employers are often referred to as ERISA policies. These policies are viewed as employee benefits and are regulated differently from long-term disability policies that we purchase on our own (more about them in the next section). While most disabilities would be covered under these policies, on-the-job injuries are covered by Workers' Compensation. I do not discuss Worker's Compensation in this book.

If you suffer a disabling event, you will generally receive a percentage of your income, ranging from 50% to 80% of your base salary. The most common coverage is 60%. If you are a senior-level executive, there might be additional financial disability benefits that you are entitled to, but for most employees, the basic disability insurance benefit applies. Generally, disability benefits do not include any type of bonus.

Your benefits typically start immediately after your short-term disability ends, which is usually six months. The premiums are either fully paid by your employer or by you. Some employer plans allow employees to buy additional coverage under the same plan at the employee's expense, which categorizes the policy as a hybrid one.

How long the Long-term disability benefit lasts will depend on the terms of your policy and will vary by employer. I spoke to someone recently who told me that her benefit was 80% of her salary. I thought that was excellent, until she told me it only lasted for three years. According to Kiplinger, the average group long-term disability claim lasts 34.6 months[1]. This means that if she is one of the unlucky people who becomes disabled and it goes beyond 3 years, she would have no income at the end of those 3 years unless she qualifies and gets Social Security Disability Income.

Ideally, both short-term and long-term disabilities should work in tandem to offer a layered lifeline with no break in income if your illness extends beyond six months. But this is more nuanced. For example, take my experience. I became ill several times during a twelve-month period.

---

[1] Are You Underestimating Your Need for Disability Insurance?" Kiplinger, September 9, 2020.

Because of the look-back provision, I had a break in income and needed to rely on my emergency fund to get me through.

LTD plans are complex, and I will not claim to know all the ins and outs, but I will break it down as best as possible in layman's terms, focusing on some of the key things to understand and practical tips to navigate the application process.

DISABILITY DEFINITIONS IN LONG-TERM DISABILITY POLICIES

The definition of *"disability"* in long-term disability policies is often easier to meet than in other types of insurance policies. This definition will vary by policy. Believe it or not but this can happen even when the policies are issued by the same insurance company. There are typically three possible types of definitions: own occupation, any occupation, and hybrids.

- **Own Occupation:** Many policies define "disability" as simply being unable to perform one's own occupation (sometimes called "regular occupation"). This definition is easiest to meet because, under this definition, you, the claimant, do not need to be totally disabled from all jobs to receive benefits. Under this definition, you only need to prove that you cannot perform the essential duties of your own occupation.

  In my case, the duties of my job required me to sit for long periods of time, attend meetings, perform in-depth research, review detailed transaction and policy documents of large corporations, and create reports and/or memoranda. Some of the symptoms of my injuries were weak, numb, and tingling hands and feet on an ongoing basis, my inability to sit or stand for long periods, and migraines. It was not feasible for me to perform my job duties. Therefore, by the definition of my policy, I was disabled.

- **Any Occupation**: Under an "any occupation" definition of disability, you must prove that you cannot perform any occupation for which you are, or may become, qualified based on education, training, and experience. This is a more difficult standard to meet. You must prove not only an inability to perform the duties of your own occupation but also an inability to perform the duties of any other reasonable occupation.

  Using my example above, if my policy defined disability using this clause, I still would have met the definition because I am still restricted from doing just about any job due to the severity of my ongoing symptoms.

  To paint a clearer picture, let's use Nancy, a brain surgeon, as an example. She becomes disabled because of pain in her hands and can no longer perform surgeries. She can, however, become a consultant with a pharmaceutical company on new drugs that they are manufacturing. While Nancy is disabled in her own occupation, by the criteria in her long-term disability policy, she is not disabled since she can work as a consultant. Her insurance company would deny her claim.

- **Hybrid:** A hybrid definition of disability combines aspects of both the "own occupation" and "any occupation" definitions. With a hybrid definition, the claimant generally must prove an inability to perform their own occupation for a specific period (for example, 18–24 months), after which they must prove they cannot perform any occupation.

  For my policy, "own occupation", or my inability to work in my profession was twenty-four months, then the definition of disability switched to "any occupation". I attempted to do my business to meet the "any occupation" definition. However, I struggled tremendously due to ongoing pain, numbness in my hands, and other chronic issues, including migraines. Eventually, my doctors decided that it was not feasible and limited me to working no more than 10 hours in any occupation.

- **Benefit Duration:** This specifies how long you will receive benefits. It can range from a set number of years, e.g., 3, 5, 10, or until retirement age. The duration of the policy through my job is through age 65.

  The supplemental policy that I purchased is a 5-year policy. This means that if I am still disabled at the end of year 5, I will no longer receive any disability income from that policy.

- **Elimination Period (Waiting Period):** This is the period between when you become disabled and when you start receiving benefits. It is vital to factor this waiting period into your financial planning. Remember that most long-term disability policies generally have a six-month waiting period. Some short-term disability policies may also have a waiting period, so check with your human resource department.

A word of caution: I believe that most of us who suffer from a disabling condition are eager to get back to our careers or do something other than sit at home relying on long-term disability insurance. Be sure that you are in a very good medical condition to go back to work and perform at a level that is optimal.

I recall someone sharing with me a story of an individual who found a job in another field under the *"any occupation"* definition because she could not live on the 60% disability income she was receiving and wanted to earn more. This individual struggled for several months in this new job and ultimately had to give up the job due to a lack of performance.

This individual now had no benefits because the ERISA plan had terminated, and she was not on the new job long enough to qualify for their long-term disability policy benefits. If you do not feel healthy enough, do not push yourself too fast. Find ways to make the income work, or if you have been cut off from your policy, fight to get back on. I will be sharing some of my personal experiences.

NAVIGATING THE MAZE: A LOOK AT DIFFERENT LTD OPTIONS

LTD benefits are not a one-size-fits-all solution. There are various plans available, each with its advantages and drawbacks. Understanding these distinctions will help you identify which benefits you need regardless of whether you are employed or self-employed. You can then use these insights to make a purchase decision. Some of the key plans that you need to be aware of include:

1. **Employer-Provided LTD (ERISA):**

    - Many workplaces offer group long-term disability insurance as a benefit. The good news is that your employer often pays the entire cost (the premium) for this insurance. These are often referred to as ERISA plans because they follow the Employee Retirement Income Security Act, a federal law enacted in 1974 that is meant to give us certain protection, including the right to file a lawsuit in the Federal Court if we are denied disability benefits that we believe we are entitled to. These plans outline specific processes to apply for benefits and file an appeal.

    - There is usually a waiting period of 6 months after you become disabled before you can begin to collect disability income. Sadly, while we would think that an ERISA policy would offer great protection, it is a mixed bag, and one might even say more detrimental. You have no say over the terms of the policy. Larger insurers have the upper hand, and because of it, they can be unscrupulous in their dealings with you.

- Since your employer pays the premium, the income that you receive will be taxed. You will also be required to pay for your medical benefits as well. Most plans only cover your base salary; therefore, if you receive a large annual bonus, none of that will be factored in, and you will pay taxes.

- For example, my company's disability insurance replaced 60% of my salary, but it did not include bonuses or other benefits. Because my employer paid the premium, the income I received was taxed. My medical benefits were also deducted.

2. **Individual (Private) LTD:**

- This is a contract between you and an insurance company where you purchase your disability policy directly from the insurance company. You would purchase a private policy if your employer's policy does not replace your income, if your employer does not offer long term disability benefits, or if you are self-employed. By working with an insurance agent, you will determine the terms that are best suited for your goals. Here is how it works:

  o **Pick Your Payout:** Decide how much of your income you want to replace if you are unable to work. You can factor in your anticipated annual bonus as part of your total income. Note that most insurance companies do not want to insure you up to 100% of your income, as they believe that may discourage you from going back to work even if you are able to. Yes, we are always looked at as having ulterior motives. Sad, but it's true!

- o **Keep Up with Rising Costs:** Many plans offer the opportunity to include in your policy the option to increase the benefits that you will receive over time. The premium will also increase, but it is a great way to keep up with inflation. You can also decide on your anniversary, when you receive the notice for the premium increases, that you no longer want to keep increasing the amount.

- o **Waiting-period Matters:** Decide how long you would wait after becoming disabled before you started receiving benefits. The shorter the wait (e.g., 3 months), the more you will pay in premiums.

- o **Underwriting:** There is an underwriting process. This means that the company will collect various types of information, such as your age, current income, occupation, and lifestyle, to determine how much coverage to offer. They will also review your medical history. Just like when purchasing life insurance, be very honest with the information that you provide to help them make the best decision.

My personal experience: I bought an individual plan that replaced close to 40% of my income and added a feature (rider) that automatically increased my benefits each year. The extra cost for this feature was minimal. I also chose a plan that starts paying me after three months of disability because I knew that my short-term disability did not pay 100% of my salary for the entire six months, and I did not want to deplete my emergency fund.

Looking back, if I were to do it again, I would have purchased a policy for at least 10 years. It removes the anxiety about not having income after year 5, because we can never truly tell how long our disabling condition will last. While I hope to be working and thriving in the next few years, who would have thought that I would still be recovering almost 3 years later?

Let's have a look at some key advantages of individual LTD policies:

- **ERISA-Independence:** Private policies are not subject to ERISA regulations, offering you more flexibility and control.

- **Guaranteed Income Protection:** These policies offer a contractual guarantee of income if you meet the criteria defining disability in your policy. You can think of them as the lifeline that will help you close the gap between what your employer offers and your total income.

- **Customization:** You can tailor your policy to your needs. This includes features like a 3-month waiting period and a 10-year benefit duration. For your employer policy, you have no options or say in the decision-making process.

- **Tax Benefits:** Because you pay your premium with after-tax dollars, the benefits that you receive are tax-free. This means that if you replace 30% of your income, since you will not be paying any taxes, the total amount of income that you receive may be on par with your pre-disability income.

- **Portability:** Your private policy remains yours regardless of job changes or unemployment. Employer-sponsored policies, on the other hand, go away once you are no longer with that company and many have a waiting period before you qualify.

- **Premium Guarantee:** You can purchase a policy that has one-level premium for the entire time that you own the policy. The premium will only change if you purchase a rider to keep up with the cost of inflation, and while I would advise against it, you can choose to discontinue paying for that rider.

- **Peace of Mind:** A private policy offers peace of mind knowing you will have financial security in case of disability, and that is priceless!

If you are self-employed or your employer does not offer long-term disability insurance, be sure to purchase a private disability policy. The agents will work with you to determine how much coverage you need. If you currently have an employer-sponsored long-term disability policy, ensure that you have enough coverage, or get a private policy to close the gap.

3. **Social Security Disability Insurance (SSDI):**

- This is a federal disability income program. It provides monthly benefits to individuals who have worked and paid into social security but can no longer work due to a disabling event. Recipients receive monthly benefits based on lifetime average earnings covered by social security, and payments generally start in the sixth month. The application process is very long, and less than a quarter of first-time applications get accepted without having to appeal.

4. **Workers' Compensation (WC):**

- This type of compensation is state-mandated and provides partial income replacement as well as medical benefits to employees who are injured on the job.

THE REALITY ON THE GROUND

Many of us rely on our employer's disability insurance benefits without knowing how much of our income is covered. Many people also do not realize that they can purchase their own private policy. I did a poll with several professionals across different income levels and age groups, asking about whether they felt prepared if they suffered a disabling event.   The most common response from the poll was that they were covered through their employer's disability policy.

Upon further inquiry, most of these individuals were surprised to discover that the average employer policy only covers 60% of their income, excluding bonuses and incentives, and that this income is reduced by taxes and healthcare benefits costs, which we must pay.

My conversation with a high-powered executive at a major tech company highlighted the deep knowledge gap. She had a difficult time opening up at first, but once she did, she was very forthcoming. She was recently divorced with two young children. She had no savings, no emergency fund, and while, steadily, she had been building a retirement plan, she said it had been wiped out due to her recent divorce. She had no idea what percentage of her income would be replaced by her disability insurance benefits. She commented a couple of times during our conversations that she would be better off dead than disabled because she had life insurance, even though it was all through her job.

I believe that conversation cuts to the core of what so many other individuals that I spoke with, and most Americans in general, are feeling. The truth is that we do not have to continue to operate from a place of fear and embarrassment. We can empower ourselves to take this knowledge and learn how to protect ourselves and our loved ones.

I want to outline some key considerations for deciding whether you need to purchase a private policy and how much coverage you need. The ideal plan for everyone will be different since it is based on your specific needs and circumstances.

Considerations		Decisions
Your employment situation: Are you self-employed?		**Yes.** You do not have coverage anywhere else, and unless you have other sources of passive income to replace your current income, or your business is self-sustaining, you will need income coming in your door once you can no longer operate your business.
Do you frequently change jobs?	**Should you purchase a private policy?**	**Yes.** Most company have a waiting period before you qualify for certain benefits, including long term disability insurance. Your private policy is yours regardless of where you work.
Financial needs: Would your employer disability policy cover your current expenses?		**Yes.** If most of us are honest, we will not be able to survive on the 60% of our income that our policy replaces. Therefore we would need a private policy to help close the gap.
Health status: Do you have any pre-existing conditions that might affect your eligibility?	**Will you get a private policy?**	The harsh reality is that, a pre-existing condition may disqualify you from purchasing a policy, or depending on the condition, the price may be higher.
Budget: Can you afford the premium for an individual LTD plan?		Let's face it. Price will be a factor in deciding what type of coverage you get. If you cannot afford it, I highly recommend that you go back to the budget chapter, and begin finding ways to cut unnecessary expenses, because if you are having financial struggles now, imagine how detrimental it would be with that reduced income.

Above all else, consulting with a financial coach or an experienced insurance agent can be very helpful in securing the right policy for you.

I recommend a financial coach for various reasons that include:

- You may not have your finances in order currently.

- Working with a coach will allow you to take a holistic look at your financial picture and identify the changes that you need to make.

- By doing the work, you will be able to identify and fix your current spending habits, create a realistic budget, manage your debt, and, if necessary, repair your credit and start putting in place other financial building blocks.

In addition, a financial coach may also be able to assist you in working through certain tax implications. These are all important components of financial planning and will help you have a better picture of the total income that you would need if you were to become disabled. Your coach will also guide you in asking the insurance agent the right question so that you end up with a policy that is beneficial to you.

If you choose to do it alone, do your research to ensure that you are asking the right questions and getting the policy best tailored to your needs. I will also caution you that, while there are many wonderful insurance agents in the industry, there are some who are just looking to make a quick buck. They may put you in the wrong policy that is not suitable for your profile, and you will not realize that until it is too late. I always tell my clients to speak to at least three agents to help inform their decision.

DECODING THE MATH: UNDERSTANDING BENEFIT CALCULATIONS, PAYOUT PERCENTAGES, AND EXCLUSIONS IN LTD PLANS

I promise you that I will try to keep this dry, boring topic as relatable as I can so that you can pick out the pieces that you need to make an informed decision. While LTD plans can be a financial lifeline in times of disability, the specifics of how much you receive and what is covered can feel like a tangled web of legalese. This section aims to demystify the numbers game and exclusions you might encounter in different LTD plans.

BENEFIT CALCULATIONS: CRACKING THE CODE

The amount of money you receive through LTD benefits is determined through a calculation specific to your plan. Here is a breakdown of some common factors that influence your benefit amount:

- **Pre-Disability Earnings:** Since most plans do not cover any discretionary bonus that you receive, you would be taking your total earnings and multiplying them by the percentage that your company offers. Let's take a simple example: if you make a $74,000 base salary, receive an annual bonus of $20,000, and then become disabled with a policy that pays 60% coverage, you will receive income based on your $74,000 base salary. If you have healthcare costs of $8,000 annually, that will be deducted from your disability income. Let's put this in a table so that you can see the difference in income.

	Income Before Disability	60% Disability Income
Salary	74,000	44,400
Bonus	20,000	-
Healthcare Benefits	(8,000)	(8,000)
Total Income	**86,000**	**36,400**
Taxes	(12,900)	(3,640)
Net Income	**73,100**	**32,760**
Monthly Net Income	**6,092**	**2,730**

We assume 15% taxes on your regular Income. For your disability income we reduce taxes to 10% because of the decrease in income.

- Notice the significant difference in income. You have gone from monthly disposable income of $6,092, if we take an average of the bonus, to $2,730 when you become disabled. That is less than half of your income. How long would you be able to survive on this, regardless of how much you cut from your budget? This is the reality of becoming disabled and relying solely on your employer's disability policy.

- ○ During my conversation with a friend recently, she informed me that her family would be able to live comfortably on 60% of her income long-term. This is not typical for most American families, so I applaud her for that. I still recommended that she learn more about how much her policy offered and consider getting a private policy as well. It is better to have more disposable income than not enough.

- **Integration with Other Benefits:** Some plans may integrate benefits from Social Security or other disability programs, reducing your LTD payout. For example, the disability insurance provided by my employer has a clause that requires that I apply for Social Security disability income. Once I get approved for this benefit, the amount of my ERISA benefits offered through my job will be reduced by the income I am receiving from social security.

As a result, in the example above, if Social Security benefits were approved for $1,200, the disability income of $2,730 that you receive from your ERISA policy would be reduced by $1,200. So, in this case, the amount you receive in total would not change, the insurance company would just be paying you less.

- **Maximum Benefit Amounts:** This sets a cap on the total monthly benefit you can receive, regardless of your pre-disability earnings. If you are a high-income earner, you want to check with your benefits office if you have a cap.

EXCLUSIONS: THE NOT-SO-FINE PRINT—NON-ERISA PLANS

It is important to remember that no LTD plan covers everything. While the specifics will vary depending on your policy, there are some general exclusions to be aware of:

Pre-existing Conditions: Most plans exclude pre-existing conditions unless they meet specific criteria. This might involve a certain period having passed since the condition was diagnosed or proof that the condition is stable and unlikely to cause a disability. Make sure to carefully review this section of your policy and ask questions if anything is unclear.

A doctor in her mid-fifties told me she was diagnosed with a medical condition, and as a result, could no longer purchase a long-term disability policy. She disclosed to the insurance company how long she has had the condition, and that it has been asymptomatic – supported by her medical records. She asked if they could write her a policy, excluding coverage for this illness and the accompanying symptoms. They concluded that she was too high a risk and declined to offer her a policy. She missed the boat on ever getting a long-term disability policy going forward.

I know that when we are young and healthy, long-term disability insurance is not top of mind. We, however, cannot ignore the social security statistics (one-in-four Americans over twenty years old will become disabled before they retire). Being able to protect ourselves will offer each of us peace of mind.

- **Other Potential Exclusions:** Some plans may also exclude disabilities caused by self-inflicted acts, substance abuse, or acts of war. It is always a good practice to review the full list of exclusions in your policy to avoid any surprises down the road.

OTHER TROUBLING CLAUSES THAT ARE COMMON IN POLICIES

These are a few examples of troubling clauses that you may find in your policy.

- Limiting your benefits for mental health issues to 24 months

- Payment is contingent only if you are unable to perform all the duties of your job

- You cannot receive disability benefits for chronic illnesses like fatigue, pain or other self-reported illnesses that cannot be verified by a diagnostic study

- You will be denied benefits if you have a pre-existing condition and were on medication within a certain period before becoming disabled

YOUR ACTION ITEMS

Understanding your benefit calculations, payout percentages, and exclusions in LTD plans can be daunting, but do not get discouraged. I want you to remember that having a clear understanding of your needs will help you make an informed decision about your LTD coverage. Before we move on to the next chapter, I want you to do the following:

- **Contact Human Resource:** Obtain a copy of your employer-provided LTD policy documents.
  - Read it thoroughly and highlight any **confusing sections** that require clarification.
  - Look specifically for:

- **Benefit amount:** How much will you receive if you become disabled?

- **Benefit duration:** How long will you receive benefits for?

- **Elimination period:** How long will the wait be before you start receiving benefits?

- **Definition of disability:** Does your policy use the "own occupation" or "any occupation" definition?

- **Exclusions:** Are there any conditions or activities that the plan does not cover?

- **Ask questions.** Create a list of questions and ask for clarification on any unclear provisions. You should not be surprised that the first person that you speak with does not know enough to guide you. Remain persistent in speaking to different individuals until you fully understand your benefits. Examples of questions to ask.

  - How much disability am I entitled to?

  - How long does it last?

  - Is there a waiting period?

- **Consult an Attorney:** If necessary, speak to an attorney that specializes in long-term disability benefits to clarify the confusing areas of your policy.

If you do not have enough coverage through your employer, consider consulting a financial coach and/or an insurance agent. They can help you assess your individual needs and recommend the best LTD coverage for you. This is particularly important for self-employed individuals, but equally as important if your employer does not offer disability insurance coverage or if you believe you cannot survive on a fraction of your income.

Getting the financial help you need in case of a disability will be easier because it will help you live the same lifestyle while navigating the disabling event.

KEY TAKEAWAYS

- This chapter focuses on short- and long-term disability (LTD) insurance and how it can financially protect you if you become disabled.

- **Short-Term Disability (STD)** provides all or a portion of your salary for temporary illnesses, typically lasting up to 6 months. Benefits and waiting periods vary by company.

- **LTD** is designed to replace a portion of your income (usually 50%–80%) if you are disabled for an extended period, potentially until retirement.

- There are two main LTD options:

  - **Employer-provided LTD (ERISA):** Often paid for by your employer, benefits may be taxable and may integrate with other disability programs, reducing your payout.

  - **Individual LTD (private):** Purchased directly from an insurance company, offering more flexibility and control over your coverage but with premiums you pay yourself. Benefits are typically tax-free.

- **Social Security Disability Insurance** and **Workers' Compensation (WC)** are also mentioned as other sources of disability income.

- **Benefit calculations:** factors like pre-disability earnings, benefit percentage, are explained.

- **Exclusions:** Plans may exclude pre-existing conditions, self-inflicted disabilities, and certain activities.

- The importance of reviewing the fine print: key terms like "definition of disability," "benefit duration," and "elimination period" are explained.

- Choosing the right policy depends on your employment situation, financial needs, health status, and budget. Consider consulting a financial coach and an insurance agent for guidance.

You made it to the end! This was a tough, but necessary, chapter. By now, you should have a good understanding of long-term disability insurance. Revisit this chapter as many times as necessary. In the next chapter, we dive directly into disability insurance as your plan B and a way to protect yourself when the crippling surprise of disability hits you. See you there!

CHAPTER 4

Get The Right Protection: **How to shop for a policy**

—Preparation, with a ready Plan B, offers the strongest shield, especially in our most vulnerable moments."

Disability insurance as a financial planning tool, is proven to be one of the best ways to protect what might be your most valuable asset—your income. When you have a disability insurance policy, you will receive a monthly income that you can use for any purpose.

If you are independently wealthy with multiple streams of passive income or have other financial resources that will cover you if you lose your income, a disability policy may not be a priority. The average American, however, cannot afford to ignore the need for income replacement if they become ill. Unfortunately, most people do not think about it until it is too late.

It may sound counterintuitive to take on an additional expense when you are barely covering your monthly bills; however, as I discussed in the previous chapter, your income can be severely reduced if you become unexpectedly disabled. This reduction can lead to great financial hardship, including bankruptcy. Effectively managing your budget can allow you to identify cash to put towards the purchase of a policy.

WHY YOUR EMPLOYER'S LTD MIGHT NOT BE ENOUGH: THE CASE FOR PRIVATE DISABILITY INSURANCE

When you start working for a company, the size of the company and the benefits it offers will typically determine whether it offers LTD benefits. As we have seen, ERISA governs these employer-offered plans. It is important to note that only a handful of states require employers to provide disability benefits to employees.

Under ERISA plans, we have little control over the contents or administration of our employer-provided policies and are at the mercy of the company. Given their profit motives, their goal is to pay out as little as possible. Even when the insurance company denies or terminates your benefits for unscrupulous reasons, you cannot sue them for bad-faith loss. There is generally no warning or grace period when your policy gets terminated.

Given these risks, having additional sources of income, or a private disability policy will help to cushion the blow. If you are self-employed, or your employer does not offer a policy, you should strongly consider purchasing your own policy.

CONSIDERATIONS WHEN PURCHASING A POLICY

Do not talk your way out of getting a policy due to lack of affordability. Go back to the chapter on budgeting and find ways to make it affordable. Once you invest in a policy, do not let it lapse. Yes, it may seem like you are just tossing money out the door, but the moment that you need it will be the moment you realize how important an investment it is. The level of stress that will be wiped away cannot be measured. It will give you time to focus on your healing.

Before you purchase a disability policy, meet with at least three agents. Educate yourself beforehand so that you can have all your questions answered and that you can ask the right questions:

Be sure to discuss the following:

- The amount of short-term and long-term disability you have and the coverage period.

- Your current income and whether you receive any type of bonus

- Any pre-existing conditions and what that might mean for getting a policy

- **Coverage and Exclusions:**

  - What types of disabilities are covered?

  - What are some specific **exclusions** that might be concerning (pre-existing conditions, certain activities)?

  - Are there any limitations on benefits, such as a maximum coverage amount or a requirement to be completely unable to work (own occupation vs. any occupation)?

- **Financial Considerations:**

  - **Disability Start Date:** What is the waiting period (elimination period) before benefits begin? This is crucial for financial planning.

  - **Benefit Amount:** How much benefit would be right for your circumstances to maintain your financial security?

  - **Premiums:** How do prices vary based on different elimination periods?

- o **Premium Waivers:** Is there a waiver available that would pause your premium payments if you became disabled?

  - o **Cost-of-Living Adjustments (COLA):** Is there a COLA rider available to adjust your benefits for inflation, and what is the additional cost?

  - o **Taxes:** Are the benefits taxable income?

  - o **Bonuses:** Do you want any portion of your bonuses covered by the disability benefits?

- **Flexibility and Portability:**

  - o **Partial Disability Coverage:** Does the policy cover scenarios where you can work in a limited capacity?

  - o **Policy Adjustments:** Can you increase your coverage amount in the future to reflect large salary increases due to job changes or inflation?

  - o **Portability:** Can you take your policy with you if you leave your current employer? The answer is usually yes.

- **Claims Process and Appeals:**

  - o **Look-Back Period:** If you become disabled twice within a defined timeframe, how will the policy handle it?

  - o **Claim Denial Appeal Process:** What steps should you take if your claim is denied? Understanding the appeals process is crucial in a dispute.

- **Additional Considerations:**

  - o **Dividends (Mutual Insurers):** If considering a mutual insurance company, inquire about potential dividends you might receive. Mutual insurers are insurance companies that are not traded on the stock market.

- o **Policy Cancellation:** Certain clauses might allow the insurer to cancel your policy. Understand the conditions that could trigger this.

- o **Rider Availability:** Are there any optional riders not already discussed?

DECIDING HOW MUCH DISABILITY INSURANCE TO GET

Let's look at an example of how you could decide on the amount and duration of your disability policy.

Imagine that Mary works for a bank and earns a $120,000 salary annually. She maintains 6 months of emergency funds, and her company pays her a 20% bonus annually. Mary's company offers both short-term and long-term disability benefits with a 12-month lookback period. Therefore, if Mary becomes ill 2 times during the year, she will only receive 6 months of short-term disability income for the entire year.

For the short-term benefits, Mary will receive 100% of her salary for the first three months. After the first three months, Mary will receive 70% of her salary. The short-term disability policy ends at the end of the twenty-six weeks.

Mary's organization also offers long-term disability. The waiting period is 6 months, and Mary will receive 60% of her base salary. She will be responsible for paying her health care costs and taxes.

All income that Mary receives will be taxable since her employer pays her insurance premium as part of her benefits package. How should Mary determine how much supplemental long-term disability she should get?

SCENARIO 1: PRIORITIZING SHORT-TERM COVERAGE

Mary considers several factors when determining her LTD needs:

- **Short-Term Disability:** Mary feels comfortable with her current short-term disability coverage.
- **Bonus Income:** Mary relies on her annual bonus ($24,000) and wants it factored into her private disability income.
- **Long-Term Disability Coverage Gap**: Her employer-provided LTD plan only replaces 60% of her salary, which means that her salary will be reduced to $72,000 annually or $6,000 monthly. To bridge the gap, she has concluded that she would like to purchase an additional $5,000 per month ($2,000 per month bonus plus $3,000 from her salary).

Mary's Decision: Based on these factors, Mary would like to purchase a LTD policy that pays at least $5,000 per month with a 3-month waiting period, since she does not want to use all of her emergency fund. She desires a 10-year coverage period.

For visual people like me, below is the breakdown of Mary's income if she becomes disabled. With the private disability coverage, her monthly income will be $11,000 instead of $12,000 in both years 1 and 2. Because she chose the 3-month waiting period, she began receiving income from her private policy within 3 months of becoming disabled. Mary would adjust her budget for the reduction in monthly income.

Another benefit that Mary has from the private policy is that she does not pay taxes on the income that she receives, so her tax liability will be reduced at the end of the year. For example, in year two, she will only pay taxes on the $72,000 from her ERISA policy. The $60,000 is tax-free. She will need to deduct her medical benefits from this income.

	Income Before Disability	
Salary	$120,000	
Bonus	24,000	
Total Income	144,000	
Monthly Income (incl. bonus)	**$12,000**	
	Year 1	**Year 2**
Short Term Disability		
100% first 3 months	$30,000	-
70% last 3 months	21,000	-
Total 6 months Income	**$51,000**	-
6 Months LTD (60% of base salary)	36,000	$72,000
Private Long term Disability ($5K/mth)	45,000	60,000
Total Income	$132,000	$132,000
Monthly Income	**$11,000**	**$11,000**

SCENARIO 2: UTILIZING EMERGENCY FUNDS & LONG-TERM DISABILITY COVERAGE

Mary considers a different approach in this scenario:

- **STD & Emergency Fund:** Since her STD plan covers 100% for the first 3 months and 70% for the next 3 months, she plans to use her emergency fund to cover the remaining 30% during those months. This allows her to consider a LTD policy with a 6-month waiting period.

- **Bonus Income Not Considered:** Mary's everyday expenses do not depend on her bonus, so she has chosen not to factor it into her LTD coverage amount.

- **LTD Coverage for Salary Gap:** She focuses on covering the 40% her employer-provided LTD does not replace and adds an additional $800 per month to cover her health insurance, which translates to a monthly benefit need of $4,800.

- **Coverage Duration:** Mary desires coverage for 5 years.

In this scenario, Mary will have lower income in both years but will be in a lower tax bracket due to the tax-free income that she is receiving from her private policy in each of these years.

	Income Before Disability	
Salary	$120,000	
Bonus	24,000	
Total Income	144,000	
Monthly Income (incl. bonus)	**$12,000**	
	Year 1	**Year 2**
Short Term Disability		
100% first 3 months	$30,000	-
70% last 3 months	21,000	-
Total 6 months Income	**$51,000**	-
6 Months LTD (60% of base salary)	36,000	$72,000
Private Long term Disability ($4,800K/mth)	28,800	57,600
Total Income	$115,800	$129,600
Monthly Income	**$9,650**	**$10,800**

Important note: Before meeting with insurance agents, consider your unique circumstances and desired coverage. This foundational knowledge empowers you to have a productive conversation with agents and explore options that align with your needs and budget. Remember, cost will also be a factor, so prepare a few scenarios based on your financial feasibility. By doing this groundwork, you approach the process with a clear understanding of your needs, will be able to ask the right questions, and therefore avoid solely relying on an agent's recommendations.

Here Is What I Did When I Purchased My Policy: I did not factor in my bonus since I never relied on it for my daily lifestyle. I decided that since my employer offered full disability coverage for only the first 3 months, I did not want to wait 6 months for my long-term disability to kick in because I did not want to use up my emergency fund. I therefore decided to get coverage that would replace my income, excluding my bonus, and elect a 3-month waiting period.

There are two of the things that I did that, in retrospect, I would have done very differently. First, I did not factor in my bonus. I generally used my bonus for vacations or any upcoming one-time expenses. I would encourage everyone to factor in their bonus if the price of your policy is still manageable. It is better to receive more than less, especially with those unexpected expenses that tend to pop up.

The second thing is that I purchased a policy for only 5 years. My rationale was that I do not think I will become disabled at an early age, so if I get disabled in my fifties and it is permanent, both policies could probably take me through 60. At 60, my children will no longer be dependent on me. With the lower expenses, I could live off the long-term disability income as well as my other resources until I begin withdrawing from my retirement plan.

Looking back, I would have purchased a policy for at least 10 years. It removes the anxiety about not having income after year 5, because we can never truly tell how long our disabling condition will last. While I hope to be working and thriving in the next few years, who would have thought that I would still be recovering almost 3 years later?

Here is another reality for LTD policies. In my experience, I believe for those long-dated disability policies, insurers will always try to find ways to terminate your policy much sooner. You must continue to prove unequivocally that you meet the disability criteria, so that even if they terminate your policy, you will have good grounds to support a reinstatement.

CHOOSING THE RIGHT DISABILITY INSURANCE COMPANY

Selecting the right disability insurer is crucial. Do your research. Go online and see what individuals with policies from the company have said. Many disability law firms also highlight cases they have won and speak about certain patterns they notice with different insurance companies. There will always be negative reviews, no matter which company, but if you are seeing an overwhelming number of negative reviews or a pattern that the law firm calls out for a particular company, then that may be a red flag. That is also why it is so important to do some homework ahead of time before meeting with an insurance agent.

My personal experience with the company from which I purchased my LTD policy has been positive (despite their extensive inquiries!). The nature of the process is that it is very intrusive, but once you get over that hurdle, the claims manager I have had for most of the process has been amazing. She is extremely transparent; she explains the process clearly, and her communication is excellent. Even when I am overwhelmed and frustrated with the requests and demands—and there are many—I have a clear understanding of what they are asking for and why. I really respect their process, and I believe that the claims manager is someone who seems to be a generally nice person.

Unfortunately, with your employer-sponsored policy, you have no choice about who will be your long-term disability carrier. The company administering my LTD policy has been an utter nightmare, and their reviews online scream it!! The staff lacks basic training and empathy. They appear to have issues with turnover and limited staff supervision. They have no process, they sow seeds of confusion, and the employees are unethical and blatantly lie. The return-to-work coordinator was the only person that I dealt with that I felt was trustworthy and transparent.

It has been a frustrating and agonizing experience, which I believe is deliberately done to kick you off long-term disability and frustrate you to the point where you want to give up. I believe we, as employees, should hold our employers to a higher standard to encourage them to choose reputable companies with a good track record of treating us with respect. I have written to my former employer several times to share my negative experiences. I doubt anything will come of it, but if more of us voice our dissatisfaction and outrage, then things may begin to change.

PROCESS FOR PURCHASING A LONG-TERM DISABILITY POLICY

Now that you have come this far and understand the benefits of having a policy, here are a few things to consider:

1. **Compare Quotes:**

   - **Get quotes from multiple insurers:** Contact at least three insurance professionals to gather quotes on individual LTD policies.

   - **Compare Apples to Apples:** Make sure each quote covers your *"must-have"* features and benefits. Pay close attention to details like benefit amounts, elimination periods, length of policy, and definitions of disability. Also, look for some of the exclusions that I discussed.

2. **Application and Underwriting:**

   - **Submit Your Application:** Once you have chosen a policy, it is time to submit your formal application. Be honest and accurate when answering health questions.

- **Underwriting Process:** The insurance company will review your medical history which will influence whether they offer coverage, the cost of the premium, or the addition of exclusions (riders) to your policy. Pre-existing conditions, especially mental health conditions, may affect your eligibility. Group LTD policies offered by your employer typically do not require individual underwriting.

Remember, Honesty Is Key. Never misrepresent your health or any other information on your application. If the insurance company discovers you were dishonest, they could deny your claim or even cancel your policy entirely. While there are some statutes of limitations, this can still happen years after you have had the policy. I will repeat this again throughout the book, because it is that important.

With policies in hand, if you are comfortable, read through them and ask the agent what each of the clauses means. If you are not comfortable, get a disability attorney to answer these questions for you — how can these be interpreted if you were to become disabled?

KEY TAKEAWAYS

- **Disability insurance is crucial:** It protects your income, your most valuable asset, in case of illness or disability.

- **Employer-provided plans may not be enough:** They are subject to ERISA, which favors insurers and provides few options for appeals of denied claims.

- **Consider a supplemental private LTD policy:** It gives you more control over your coverage and allows you to sue the insurer for bad faith denial.

- **Educate yourself before purchasing a policy:** Understand the key terms and ask questions about coverage, exclusions, benefits, and the claims process.

- **Don't skimp on coverage:** Consider factors like your income, bonus, expenses, and desired coverage duration.

- **Choose a reputable insurer:** Research the company's track record and customer reviews.

- **Don't let a policy lapse:** Maintain your coverage by identifying ways in your budget to allow you to afford it.

- **Shop around and compare quotes:** Get quotes from multiple insurers to find the best coverage for your needs and budget.

- **Work with a financial advisor or disability attorney:** They can help you assess your needs and understand the policy details.

One step at a time, we are making progress. You have come a long way, nailing down everything you need to know about disability insurance—how you can purchase a policy, how much coverage you actually need, and some red flags to look out for when purchasing a policy. You also understand why it's essential to not just buy a policy but to keep it in force.

With everything you know by now, you should be feeling a lot less intimidated by the unknowns of LTD and how to navigate it. There is still a lot to learn, and one of those is what the next chapter dives into: how to actually build your case for your benefits and how to communicate, document, and understand the content of your policy. Grab a nice drink and relax into this, paying attention to every word in the next chapter.

CHAPTER 5

Securing Your Benefits: Give Them What They Need

—Success lies in the meticulous details, each one a deliberate brick in the grand construction of achievement."

Speaking from my own experience, when I became disabled, my priority was trying to heal so that I could move on with my life and all the things I had coming down the pike. The last thing I wanted to think about was the insurance company, doctors, and the mountains of accompanying paperwork. Sadly, this is a real and necessary part of the disability process. Whether we like it or not, it must be done, and the sooner we get it over with, the better.

Why? Because that is the beginning of the process for claiming our disability income. Here is a word of advice. If you are unable to handle this on your own, I highly recommend that you designate someone to assist you. You should do this as a matter of long-term planning. This way, you do not have to worry about missing important deadlines.

When my aunt became ill, I was charged with handling most of her financial matters. The problem is that I had very little knowledge about her finances. So, I spent quite a bit of time trying to piece things together. About a year after her illness began, we discovered that she had another long-term disability policy. When we contacted the insurance company, the statute of limitations for filing a claim had already expired. They denied her the ability to file the claim based on what was written in the contract. She could have appealed that decision, but with all our time being so limited and focused on helping her heal, we never got around to appealing, and her family lost out on that income.

One of the first things that you should do once you have suffered a disabling event is to call your Human Resources office. Notifying your team or manager that you are sick is not enough; while it's courteous to talk about your illness, you are not required to discuss it with your manager or anyone on your team. Hop on a call with your Human Resource office and discuss your time out of the office with them. They will share with you the benefits that you have and the process for filing your claim, and they will inform your managers.

While I would expect that most companies will do this, if your organization does not, please get everything in writing. Review the email thoroughly and follow up on anything that is unclear and on all items that require your attention. Little details that do not seem important now, could be a big deal later. If you have private disability insurance benefits, give them a call as well to understand your benefits, especially if you already know that this event will be long-term. It is never too early to start understanding the process.

DEFINING YOUR DISABILITY

A critical aspect of securing both STD and LTD benefits hinges on building a strong case that documents the nature and extent of your disability. This often starts during the STD phase, laying the groundwork for a potential LTD claim if your recovery takes longer than anticipated. Here is what you need to know about documenting your disability and navigating communication with employers, doctors, and disability companies.

The first step is to understand the type of disability you are facing. Some of the key distinctions that you need to be aware of include:

- **Physical vs. Mental:** Your disability can be physical (back injury, chronic illness) or mental (depression, anxiety) or both. Both require proper documentation from your medical provider for you to qualify for benefits.

- **Temporary vs. Permanent:** As discussed earlier, STD typically covers temporary disabilities that generally last up to six months. Long-term disability, as its name implies, is for illnesses that are expected to last for a longer duration or even permanently.

Many disabilities that start out as short-term will end up progressing to the long-term. Similarly, as I have learned over time, many disabilities that start out as physical disabilities end up becoming both physical and mental. Be mindful of your mental state as you are going through this process, and if you find yourself becoming mentally impaired, seek professional help, document it, and add it to your file with the insurance company. They may also require you to complete additional documentation.

About a year and a half after the accident, as my anticipated speedy recovery was looking more and more distant, it started taking a mental toll. I recall speaking with my case manager in charge of my private policy, and I would mention it a few times but never submit a claim. My optimism was still strong about returning to work. This went on for a few months, until one day, while speaking with her, she asked if I planned to submit a claim because it appeared that I needed to. I had already been in therapy for several months. I eventually submitted the documentation. This meant that when my case was being periodically reviewed by the insurance companies, they had to contact my mental health therapists as well. Similarly, if other physical issues arise while you are on disability, you should include them, so that you are fully covered for all medical conditions. Some insurance policies may have clause that does not allow you to add on additional illnesses.

What that means is that even if you recover to a point where you can work physically but, due to your mental state, are unable to work, you cannot be forced to return to work. In my case, I suspect that I will recover mentally before I recover physically, so the mental health piece may not be as significant. For someone else, however, mental health may be a material factor. Do not ignore it.

- **Hybrid Disability:** If you believe that you can work part-time or with accommodations, you and your employer can decide on a schedule. That may mean that you are only on short-term disability part-time while receiving your full income for the remainder of the time. Before the car accident, while I was on short-term disability, I had medical accommodations through my job. I went from full disability to working 3 days per week over several months, until I resumed my role full-time. I received my full salary for the three days and my short-term disability income for the 2 days that I did not work.

BUILDING YOUR MEDICAL EVIDENCE

Here is what I will emphasize over and over: obtaining and providing robust medical evidence is the cornerstone of your disability claim. Be prepared to work with your medical providers to complete many forms. Your employer or the insurance company wants to confirm that you are in fact disabled over the short or long term and will require ongoing certification. Your medical providers may not be very happy about filling out paperwork and providing documentation, so you will sometimes have to have forceful conversations, including letting them know that your income will be completely cut off if they do not do their job by providing these documents. When you are building medical evidence, these are some considerations:

- **Keep Your Doctor Informed:** Clearly explain your job duties and how your disability impacts your ability to perform them. Never downplay your symptoms, because they will only work against you in the long run.

- **Functional Capacity Evaluation:** Some insurers may require an independent assessment by a healthcare professional who will evaluate your physical or mental capabilities to perform your job duties. Both Social Security and my no-fault auto insurance required an independent medical exam. This is where a medical provider of their choice will examine you after reviewing your treatment record. They will decide whether you are in fact disabled.

- **Comprehensive Medical Records:** When you are in the short-term disability phase, your employer will require ongoing medical records. Ensure that your doctors are maintaining correct documentation by reviewing your file. This will help to build the records that you will need for your long-term disability claim. Do not trust that your medical provider will accurately document your case. Babysit them and be annoying if you must but ensure that all your symptoms and your diagnosis are properly documented.

I have had doctors write incorrect information in my medical record multiple times. Initially, I did not pay attention to my records. For any request that was made, I would let my medical provider know to send the information to the insurance company without even reading it. At some point I requested the records on my own and was shocked at some of the incorrect information that was included.

Let me share an example. I received steroid shots for my cervical spine. After the first shot, which was badly administered, I developed sharp shooting pain up my shoulder and down my already numb arm, and I experienced severe migraines daily. The pain was so severe that I would often scream spontaneously. I described the issue in detail to both the doctor and staff, both by phone and in person, and they even observed me going through one of the spells. Yet, in my medical records, they noted that my initial symptoms had improved by 40%.

Getting them to fix it was not a simple task because they said they could not change what was already written in my medical records! They eventually wrote an amendment. After that blatant misrepresentation of my injuries, I began requesting and reviewing all records from my providers before they were sent to the insurance company.

In another example, my physical therapist put in my record that I was injured from bench pressing fifteen pounds and that the injuries happened in 2023. I have never bench-pressed anything in my life and therefore never told them this. They would later admit that they inadvertently mixed up my file with someone else's. Although it was corrected and resent to my long-term disability insurance companies, the damage was already done. While the company that administers my private disability policy immediately saw that it was an error and treated it as such, the unscrupulous insurance company that administers my ERISA policy continued to latch on to it as fact and identified it as a key piece of evidence to terminate my policy (more on this later). I cannot stress this enough. Review your file for accuracy before it is submitted anywhere.

EMPLOYER INVOLVEMENT IN STD AND MEDICAL RECORDS

During the STD phase, your employer will require:

- **Doctor's Confirmation of Disability:** Your employer will require a doctor's note confirming your disability and its impact on your ability to work.

- **Submission of Medical Records:** You will need to submit your medical records to a designated third-party administrator or directly to your employer, depending on their policy. Check your company's STD policy for specific requirements regarding medical record submissions.

- **Return to Work:** Your employer will ask your doctor about your ability to return to work and ask them to provide a return-to-work date. All future updates to your employer will require you to provide an estimated return-to-work date. If the doctor is unsure, they will state that a return-to-work date is unknown.

Although you may be focused on recovery, collecting documentation early is crucial to building a solid foundation for your disability claim. Maintain a list of all your doctors, the dates of your visits, and your medications. This will make the process less daunting. Once there are indications that your disability will extend beyond the six-month mark, your employer will notify you to contact the long-term disability insurer.

TRANSITIONING TO LONG-TERM DISABILITY

- The intake process for long-term disability will start a few weeks before the six-month mark. Be sure to follow up and stay on track of all requests if you want to have a seamless transition. The documentation required is extensive, so allow yourself time to complete it or get someone to assist you as needed.

- The first thing that they will do is ask you to provide a list of all your medical providers, and to sign a release form to authorize the doctors to release the information. Many companies outsource the document request to a third party. Some medical providers will have strict criteria and require additional forms to be completed before releasing any of your medical records.

- They will then request medical records from all physicians, specialists, and any other healthcare professionals involved in your treatment.

UNDERSTANDING LTD CLAIM REVIEW PROCESSES AND TIMELINES

This section will give you a clear picture of what to expect during the typical claim review process and the timelines involved with LTD claims.

THE JOURNEY OF YOUR CLAIM

So, you have indicated that you need to file an LTD claim. Now, it takes a little trip through the insurance company's process. Let us break down the main stops along the way:

- **They will interview you:** Your claims manager will have an in-depth discussion with you about your claim. These calls may be recorded. They will cross-reference this information with medical records and any other information that they are able to gather.

- **Pre-existing condition:** Based on your LTD policy, they may require you to complete a pre-existing condition form where you will need to provide a list of all doctors and pharmacies that you visited within a certain timeframe. The result of this investigation will determine if you will be entitled to benefits. Insurance companies never want to pay out and will do anything they can to succeed in not paying.

- **Claims Packet:** The forms that you need to complete could be over twenty pages long. This packet will outline your action items, special reminders and rules that you must follow to avoid not being qualified for your benefits among other things. While you need to go through the document thoroughly, be sure to read the special reminder section and the section on how your benefits with your employer will change.

- **Gathering More Info (if needed):** Sometimes, the insurance company might need additional information to make their decision. They might ask for additional medical records or speak directly to a medical provider to get the full picture.

- **The Big Decision:** A team of experts, including doctors, specialists, and claims adjusters, will review all the information gathered. Based on their assessment, they will either approve or deny your claim.

THE ALL-IMPORTANT TIME FACTOR

The timeframe for processing any LTD claim can vary depending on the complexity of your case and the specific insurance company. However, here is a general idea of what to expect:

- **Initial Review:** This typically takes a few weeks (around 4-6 weeks).

- **Gathering Information:** This stage can be variable, depending on the need for additional records or consultations and how quickly your doctors respond. It could range from a few weeks to a few months.

- **Evaluation and Decision:** Once all the information is gathered, the final decision on your claim might take another few weeks.

It is important to note that these are just average timeframes. Some claims might be resolved much faster, while others might take longer, especially if there are complications or disagreements. When I filed my ERISA long-term disability claim, I began the process about 2 weeks before my benefits kicked in. We had some back-and-forth follow-up questions about the application, which took about a month. I should have also foreshadowed some challenges to come with this company, but I thought they were just part of the process. During the review process, I dealt with several different claims managers who clearly had not communicated with the previous person handling my case nor read my files. Their lack of knowledge and due diligence was obvious.

For my private policy, the initial claims manager left my case dormant as she was working on transitioning to a new job. All my messages went unanswered. While I wasn't explicitly told this, I believe she assumed that I was lying about my injuries. The company had surveyed my social media accounts and any other public information they could find. Once this new claims manager came on board, she did not beat around the bush. She began asking more questions about my business and travels.

I had not disclosed in any level of detail that I had been working on my business prior to the accident. My new claims manager dug deep into trying to understand what I was doing and how much time I was spending doing it. She then had me fill out a secondary questionnaire and write a summary of what I do in my business. We also had an in-depth conversation about my travels and how I could travel while being injured. She also requested to speak to the primary doctor that I was seeing after the accident.

Eventually, after all their questions and digging, both insurance companies concluded that I met the disability definition, and I was approved.

FINALLY APPROVED

Let's talk about the length of time both policies took before I could receive a check.

For my private policy, the entire process took about four months. My ERISA policy was approved approximately three months after I started the process.

The income that you receive will be based on the date your disability policy took effect. However, while you are waiting, you will need to have a financial cushion available to cover that period until you are approved. The reality is that the only income that I received for that entire period, from the date of my accident through the approval, was the two weeks of short-term disability income from my employer in September and the $2,000 per month that I received from my auto insurer for five months. Everything else had to be covered by my emergency fund and other resources.

As you are reading this book, and trying to decide if you really need to take on another expense, ask yourself these questions. How long will I be able to live without my income, and would the income from my ERISA policy (likely 60% of my income) be enough? If the answer is no, this is your wake-up call to start building your emergency fund and identify money in your budget to purchase a private policy.

STAYING ON TRACK

Here are some tips to help your claim move smoothly through the process:

1. **Submit complete and accurate documentation.** Ensure your claim form is completed correctly and that all required medical records are included if you are required to provide them. If the requests are sent directly to your providers, follow up with them to discuss timing. Remind them that if they do not submit your records on time, your disability income could be discontinued. I had to remind my providers several times.

2. **Respond promptly to requests.** Do not delay in providing any additional information the insurance company requests.

3. **Maintain communication.** Keep a clear line of communication with the claims manager handling your case. Let them know if you will need additional time.

4. **Seek professional guidance.** If your claim is denied, I would highly recommend consulting a lawyer that specializes in long term disability insurance.

POSSIBLE OUTCOMES: APPROVAL, DENIAL, OR DELAY

There are three possible outcomes to the claim review process:

- **Approval:** This is the best-case scenario, where the insurance company accepts your claim and begins issuing monthly benefits.

- **Denial:** If your claim is denied, you have the right to appeal the decision. This may involve submitting additional documentation. **Get an attorney!**

- **Delay:** Sometimes, the insurance company might request additional information or clarification before deciding. This might extend the review timeframe. For example, like I discussed, I had to provide information about my business, which delayed the process even longer.

HOW TO BE PREPARED WHEN DEALING WITH DISABILITY INSURANCE

There is an undeniable level of stress that comes with being on long-term disability. Just the mere fact that you are totally dependent on a company that can yank your income away with no notice can send your anxiety level soaring. Couple that with your illness and the fact that you cannot live the life you used to live, and you can easily slump into depression.

Once you start the long-term disability claims process, you will be assigned a case/claims manager who will be your point of contact. They are the ones that interview you, asking questions about how you are doing, your daily life, and how any type of therapy or other treatment is progressing. They will also ensure that your medical records are complete for review.

As with any job, you are going to have employees who do their jobs very well and those who do not. Some case managers communicate primarily by email, while others will speak to you at length. For example, I had one case manager that I never spoke with during the entire time that she was my case manager. I also had one who communicated only by email and was extremely slow to follow up, to the point that I had to escalate the issue to higher-level management. Finally, I had a third case manager who was in constant communication, explained everything clearly, and would even email a follow-up to our conversation, including next steps. She was fantastic, and she truly made the process much less anxiety driven.

One of the most crucial tips I can offer about working with your case manager is to always respond as quickly as you can. If they send you a request without a deadline, create one yourself or inquire about the due date. Your long-term disability insurer will require you to submit ongoing medical documentation supporting your disability.

If they are reviewing your case and you do not have all the requested documents, they can decide to pause paying your policy until your file is complete. Your policy likely includes language stating that it is your responsibility to ensure the insurance company has all the information it needs to review your case. This means that even if your doctors are unresponsive (and many times they are), it is up to you to follow up with them. A good case manager should notify you if they are having challenges with any request.

A word of caution: Your case manager is not your friend. Regardless of how friendly, warm, or empathetic they seem, they are still working for the insurance company. Anything you disclose to them can be used against you in the future because they are taking copious notes.

Always remember that while you obviously want to be honest with them, you may not want to volunteer any unnecessary information. It is a balancing act. Be truthful but avoid providing unnecessary details; they could be used to deny your claim later.

ONGOING REQUESTS AND HOW TO KEEP YOUR DISABILITY FROM GETTING CUT OFF

Once you are approved for your benefits, do not let your guard down. Provide all the proof for the ongoing request that will keep your disability in good standing. This will involve submitting updated records for all medical providers, answering questionnaires related to daily living, and even attending "independent" medical exams and field interviews.

These insurers are also monitoring your daily activities, including your social media accounts. All this is part of their assessment in determining whether you continue to meet the disability definition and whether you should continue to receive benefits.

Some insurance companies invest in surveillance—videos, photos, and stalking your social media—hoping to catch you doing things they can use to cut off your benefits. Find a balance between living your life and being mindful of your activities. Get an attorney if you feel like it is becoming overwhelming. If I had to do it all over again, I would probably have retained my attorney to continue any ongoing communications with them after my policy was terminated the first time.

PROCEDURES TO SATISFY INSURERS

Insurance companies will expect you to follow through with the medical procedures doctors recommended, even if there's no guarantee of success and there are more conservative treatment options recommended by other doctors. Exercise caution and not willingly bend to their pressure, because you will have to live in your body for the rest of your life. Also review the language in your policy because insurers are starting to insert more and more clauses to force you to undergo surgery or lose your benefit.

I spoke about the botched steroid shots earlier. While I was in pain, and needed some relief, I felt forced into taking the shots to satisfy my insurers. A few months later when I said no to a spinal fusion surgery and opted for a more conservative approach, my ERISA long-term disability insurer immediately began reviewing my case -- despite having just reviewed and reinstated my policy. They ultimately decided to terminate my policy for the second time in less than one year. I will share more about the termination in the next chapter.

My decision not to undergo the surgery was based on consultation with other neurosurgeons. They strongly advised against the surgery. They did not believe that I would gain the desired result and felt that the benefit did not outweigh the long-term consequences that could arise.

While the insurance company can invoke their rule that you should be under the most appropriate care for the condition causing your disability, they cannot force you to undergo surgery if the risks outweigh the benefits. They can however find ways, including lying, to terminate your benefits.

To accelerate my healing, I went to an Ayurvedic treatment center in India, which resulted in about 70% relief from the migraines and nerve pain caused by the steroid shots. Realizing how beneficial that treatment was, I decided to continue therapy and made plans to return to India in about six months. This was fully supported by my therapists and my second-opinion neurosurgeon. After the harrowing experience from the steroid's shots, any decision that I made medically would be completely independent of the insurance company's expectations to satisfy their so-called requirements.

FIELD INTERVIEWS

Some insurers may perform field interviews where a representative comes to your home, or you meet somewhere neutral, and they ask you questions to better understand your injuries and progress, and let's be frank, to see if you are lying. The representative conducting the interview will ask you to come prepared with certain items, such as your medication and list of doctors.

My understanding is that prior to or sometimes after the field interview, the company surveils you, also known as staking out your home and your social media page. They will use the data gathered to compare it to what you are telling them. For example, if you say I cannot do any yardwork, but they saw you 2 days ago during their surveillance doing yard work, they will say you are not being truthful. Some individuals choose to have their attorney present with them for these visits.

My private disability insurer requested a field visit, which I welcomed. At the time of my visit, I still could not sit for longer than half an hour without having to prop myself up with pillows. I also sometimes struggled to stand up without having to hold on to something. Between the brain fog and some of the physical challenges I was having, there was no way to second guess my symptoms.

The representative was very pleasant and had many questions. He had a keen interest in my travels and even requested for a copy of my passport, which I declined to provide. You can say no if you think they are crossing the line. For me, travel is a way to feel like I have maintained some pieces of my life. It does not mean that I am not in pain. A change of scenery does something different for the mind and body. A word of caution, however, if you want to remove some of the scrutiny, don't post your vacation pictures on social media like I did.

I told the representative that I want no part of this disability and just need to go back to the full, rich life that I led before the accident. We talked about my hobbies and the things I can no longer do. I knew that he had viewed my social media site prior to the visit because we spoke about some of my trips, so I suggested that he revisit my page and look at some of my older posts compared to the ones since the accident to see the difference in the pictures I posted. No more crazy adventures.

I also told him that I sweep my yard and put the garbage out, and that sometimes the garbage weighs more than the ten pounds I am allowed to lift, but I don't always have help, and I don't have the funds to pay someone each garbage day.

What I took away from that one-hour interaction was that the insurance company wants to understand, overall, if you are just faking it. I was very happy to have that visit because he got to see firsthand some of my daily challenges.

SEPARATING FROM YOUR EMPLOYER

Some employers will hold your position for a certain timeframe and still require you to provide ongoing certification of your disability, including your expected return to work date, if known. When I was about one year into my disability, my doctor recommended another procedure and at least two more surgeries. Recognizing that there was no possibility of returning to work in the near term, my employer and I mutually agreed at that time to separate.

Each person will handle this separation decision differently, so be prepared because it could be a very emotional period. Truth be told, I had been ready to move on from my job for quite some time before the accident. Yet, it was still difficult to accept that I did not have a job and no real prospect of what I would be doing in the immediate future. Although I had been working on building my business, it was becoming increasingly difficult to keep up with the pace. This is the period when anxiety and depression can really start ramping up, so be gentle with yourself, take time out to listen to yourself, and seek therapy if necessary.

KEY TAKEAWAYS

- **Act Quickly:** Start collecting documentation and notifying your employer and insurance company as soon as you become disabled.

- **Gather medical evidence:** Detailed medical records are essential for proving your disability. Ensure your doctors document your diagnosis, treatment plans, limitations, and restrictions. Be persistent and follow up to ensure accuracy in your records.

- **Understand Your Policies:** During your short-term disability phase, familiarize yourself with the long-term disability process and requirements of your employer and private insurance company.

- **Prepare for the Long Haul:** The long-term disability application and approval process can take months. Be patient and persistent in following up with requests.

- **Stay Organized:** Maintain a list of doctors, medications, and all disability-related documents.

- **Communicate Effectively:** Respond promptly to requests from your case manager and insurance company. Be honest but avoid oversharing unnecessary details.

- **Prepare for field interviews:** Insurance companies may send a representative to your home to assess your condition. Be prepared to answer questions and provide documentation.

- **Maintain a Financial Cushion:** The approval process can take time. It is crucial to have savings to cover your expenses until you start receiving disability benefits.

We have laid down a solid overview of building your case, the review process, and understanding your policy, and the outcomes to expect from the review. Next, we will get into how to deal with insurance companies—what to look out for, and how to fight for what is yours. See you in the next chapter.

CHAPTER 6

They Will Chew Your Up & Spit You Out: Fight for What's Yours

—The most insidious deceit often wears the cloak of kindness, hiding its true nature behind a mask of goodwill."

JUMPING OUT OF THE BOOKS TO REAL LIFE: HOW THESE COMPANIES REALLY WORK

Another doctor's appointment, another grueling choice. Spinal fusion or disc replacement_ either way, it's major surgery, and the worst part_ there were no guarantees that the numbness in my hand and the ongoing migraines would go away. As I pull off the highway to wake up my numb foot for the second time in my 70-minute drive, I miss a phone call from my claims manager. She was aware of my appointment and that I would likely be recommended to have surgery, so I figured that she was just checking in.

As I slowly pulled into my driveway, listening to her message, I was shocked to hear a voice void of emotion notifying me that my long-term disability has been discontinued, effective immediately. This was two days before I was scheduled to receive my next long term disability income check. It was soul-crushing.

THE ALLURE OF PROFIT

Insurance companies, like all businesses, operate within a range of motivations, with profit-seeking being one of the main drivers. Insurance companies' collect payments from customers who buy insurance (premiums) and aim to give their owners a meaningful return on their investment. By denying claimants or paying as little as possible, they generate more profit. The insurance company's goal optimizes profitability while balancing how much risk they are exposed to. Ultimately, they want to ensure that they make a profit.

There are many reputable, highly rated insurance companies in the U.S., but that doesn't mean they won't play hardball when it comes to paying out claims. Remember, profit is their lifeblood, and every claim they pay is money out of their pockets.

Insurance companies will scrutinize everything and look for reasons to deny or discontinue your coverage. As my case highlights, they will lie or drag out the claims or appeals process, hoping you will get discouraged and give up. Never cave. Never stop your fight.

Before an insurance company sells individual or group policies, they perform their own calculations about how much they expect to pay out. To make their decision, they use different models and factors, such as:

- **Age:** Younger people are generally healthier, although if they engage in riskier activities, they may be considered to have higher risks.

- **Job:** A construction worker has a higher chance of getting injured than someone who works in an office.

- **Health history:** If you already have a health condition, you might be more likely to have a disability in the future.

- **Habits:** Do you smoke? That can raise your risk of some disabilities.

- If their estimates are off, they may need to pay more than anticipated, thus reducing their profit!

Here is how they try to avoid selling unprofitable contracts:

- **Reviewing applications carefully:** For private policies, they review your health and job history, among other criteria, to see if you are a good fit for their policies and to determine the prices they will charge. Group policies are priced differently, factoring in size and age of group. Since these are renewable policies, they can change the price when the policy is up for renewal based on their payout experience.

- **Reviewing claims closely:** When someone says they are too hurt to work, the company performs due diligence, as described in earlier chapters, to approve or deny your claim.

- **Helping people get better:** Some companies offer rehabilitation or job training programs. This is a win-win because the person can go back into the workforce, and the company no longer must pay the disability benefits.

Insurance companies have a legal duty to follow through on their promises to policyholders (that is, their liability). If they deny a valid claim, we can sue them. It can be a long and expensive process.

YOU ARE DENIED. NOW WHAT?

When your ERISA long-term disability claim is denied, you have the right to file an administrative appeal

This does not involve a hearing. Rather, the file is referred to an appeals representative at the insurance company, who will decide the fate of the claim. They may also have "independent physicians" conduct a peer review. These *"independent physicians"* are being paid by the insurer, so don't expect their opinion to be in your favor.

I recall having to do independent medical examinations for my auto insurer. Only one out of the about 12 doctors that I saw over a period of 2 years felt that I needed additional therapy, and he only recommended therapy for six additional weeks. Even when I could barely walk, had a torn rotator cuff, and still couldn't turn my neck to the right, those doctors determined that I was fine and could go back to work. Neither of my LTD insurance companies have ever requested an independent medical exam.

When your claim is denied on appeal, you can file a lawsuit against the insurance company in Federal District Court if the coverage provided is an employee benefit subject to ERISA. The judge will have the power to grant benefits or remand the case back to the insurer for further consideration.

As we've discussed, some insurance companies will use every trick in the book, including outright lying, to deny or discontinue your disability income benefits. You must be proactive and don't go it alone, no matter how expensive it may seem.

APPEALING A DENIAL

Common Reasons for Disability Claim Denial and Policy Cancellation

Insurance companies will deny or terminate a policy claim for various reasons. Some of the most common reasons are:

Claim Denial:

- **Misinterpretation or Ignoring of Evidence:** Claims representatives are human and can make mistakes or misinterpret information, but they also have a vested interest in closing out a case. I do not know if they receive a performance bonus based on the number of cases they close, but if they are paid a bonus based on the company's performance, then I don't think it would be a stretch to say that they would want to deny or terminate as many cases as possible. Review your denial letter carefully. Make a list of any errors or misrepresentations you find, such as omissions of your medical evidence or incorrect interpretations of your limitations.

- **Lack of Sufficient Medical Evidence:** To win your disability claim, you need strong medical evidence documenting the extent and severity of your condition and how it directly prevents you from working. Your insurance company will ask you for a treatment plan. Be certain to work with your doctor to put one in place, if you do not already have one. Incomplete or insufficient evidence will lead to a denial or termination.

- **Exaggerating Your Symptoms:** As a rule of thumb, if you have a disability claim, consider that you are always monitored. If a claims manager suspects you are exaggerating your symptoms, they may initiate surveillance to verify your claim. Honesty is crucial throughout the process. That being said, we have a life to live, so balance that with trying to do reasonable things that you love while you heal. Speak to your doctor about what your limitations are and do your best to stay within them. I was surveyed by the two long term disability companies and the auto insurance company as well.

I still traveled — I wanted to meet my 50-country goals, I still posted about my trips on social media; I did this partially because I didn't want these companies controlling me, and because I just wanted to live my life in this modified way the best I could. I knew that if they observed me for even a short period, they could not deny that I struggle physically. **I would not advise you to do what I did.** They can cherry pick what evidence they want to use to build a story against you.

- **Perceived Improvement in Your Condition:** Insurance companies may deny or terminate benefits if they believe your condition has improved. Be prepared to address any perceived improvements with your doctor and provide updated documentation if necessary.

I highly recommend that if you are denied benefits, or your policy is terminated, that you seek out a long-term disability attorney. You can go it alone, but you run the risk of not having your policy reinstated. I will discuss attorneys in detail later.

Policy Cancellation: Policy cancellation can occur for several reasons, even after benefits have begun. Here are some reasons:

- **Non-payment of premiums:** This is one of the most common reasons for the cancellation of any insurance policy. Since your employer is paying for your ERISA policy, it only applies to private policies. Pay your premiums on time to avoid jeopardizing your coverage. I would also strongly advise that when you purchase a private policy, it includes a rider that stops your premium payments for as long as you are collecting disability income from that policy.

- **Material misrepresentation:** If you provided false or misleading information on your application, the insurer may cancel your policy. This can happen even if you have had a policy for a couple of years. If you file a claim, and during their investigation, they discover that you misrepresented material information, they will cancel the policy and refund you the premium that you paid. I cannot stress this enough; honesty is vital from the start.

- **Engaging in activities that significantly increase your risk of disability:** This could be relevant for certain high-risk occupations or hobbies not disclosed in the application. Be transparent about your activities to ensure proper coverage.

- **Reaching the policy's maximum benefit payout period:** Some LTD plans have a set time frame for benefit payments, and the policy terminates once that period is reached. For example, if I remain disabled, at the end of year five, I will no longer receive benefits from my private policy since the duration of the policy is five years. It is technically not a cancellation; its term has expired.

- **Policy expiration:** Some LTD policies are designed to cover you until a certain age (e.g., 65) and then expire. Be aware of your policy's end date.

A claim denial or termination should not be the end of the road. You have a right to appeal a decision. Appeal timelines vary by state and plan, but generally allow 60–180 days to submit your appeal.

If you do not have a financial cushion during the time of the appeal, this already stressful process will start to take a toll. What I would encourage you to do, is that while you are collecting your long-term disability, you identify ways to cut back and create a financial cushion. The worst part about the denial or termination is that you do not get a warning.

If the company decides you are no longer disabled, whether they are right or wrong, your benefits will stop immediately. Based on my two experiences of benefit terminations, I believe this company intentionally closes cases just before the next payment period to avoid making that payment.

TWICE TERMINATED: MY FIGHT FOR BENEFITS

If you think having your policy denied is frustrating, imagine being kicked off disability twice during the same year, by the same insurance company — the company that is providing the largest percentage of your disability income. My private policy was never denied or terminated. I spoke before about my experience with both companies. They were evaluating me during the same period and received the same doctor's information, which effectively means they would be using the same evidence.

The company administering my ERISA policy did not attempt to review all the evidence. While the insurer of my private policy notified me if they were having challenges getting information from my doctors, and worked with me to get that information, the company administering my ERISA policy used incomplete information to make their decision, and blatantly lied.

In the letter notifying me of the termination of benefits, they referenced two doctors by saying both doctors responded to their request stating that they do not have records for me for the period under review. These were two of my key providers. The truth is that they never made a request from one of the providers, and for the second one, they sent a letter withdrawing the initial request. In the letter they informed my provider that they had all the information that they needed, and no additional information was required. My doctor shared a copy of the letter with me.

When my disability benefit was terminated for the first time, I thought about appealing on my own. It was a clear-cut case. I was scheduled to do major surgery, which is a clear indication that I was still not recovered from my injuries and could not work in my or any other profession.

I knew that if I hired an attorney to represent me, it would be costly. I was not in a position mentally to go through this fight alone, and knowing how untrustworthy this company has proven itself to be, I did not want any surprises when it came to reinstating my policy. I also felt that having an attorney would demonstrate to them that I am not willing to back down, and I have someone in my corner who knows the laws. While giving up a large chunk of my income would be financially difficult, I felt that it was a worthwhile tradeoff.

THE APPEALS PROCESS

Having your disability benefits denied or prematurely terminated can be incredibly stressful. However, there are laws in place that mandate an appeals process, providing a path to challenge these decisions.

I believe many of the current rules are due for serious reform, but I fear the big dollars of the powerful industry lobbyists will make any near-term hope for change a pipe dream. Here is my advice you to:

- **Consult an attorney:** As I just described, while you can go it alone, it is best to consult with an attorney so that you understand your options. If you go it alone, make sure you have a deep understanding of all the ins and outs of the process.

- **Be mindful of deadlines:** You will typically have 90 to 180 days to file an appeal. Try to start the process as soon as possible to reduce the length of time it takes. If you decide to use an attorney, they will request:

  - The complete file that was used by the insurance company to make the decision.

  - The resume of any medical or vocational professional at the insurance company who reviewed your files to make the determination.

  - Your medical records from all your providers.

  - Submit an "appeals memo" along with the medical records to support your case.

If the attorney has not been able to collect all the medical evidence, they may ask for additional time, which the insurer has sole discretion to grant. They may also include in the memo that they reserve the right to provide additional evidence. My attorneys requested extra time during the first appeal, but it was denied despite it taking weeks for the insurance company to get the requested materials over to my attorney.

Whether you go it alone or use an attorney, be sure that you are providing all the evidence to support your case. Medical records, specialist opinions, and witness statements supporting your disability can significantly improve your chances of success.

HOW LONG WILL IT TAKE THE INSURER TO APPROVE OR DENY YOUR CLAIM OR APPEAL?

Once the insurance company receives the Appeals Memo and supporting medical records, they typically have 45 days to review the information and respond. If they need additional time, they can extend it by an additional 45 days. So, the total time from denial to reinstatement is approximately 180 days – the 90 days you must submit the memo and the 90 days they must respond.

In my first case, a decision was made about 25 days after the appeals memo was submitted. For my second case, it took over 113 days, and the company decided to maintain their decision that I no longer qualify for long term disability benefits. When the company had reached the 90-days mark, I inquired about what is our recourse. The attorney felt we should just wait, because its expensive and time consuming to file a lawsuit to compel them to respond.

These insurance companies are aware that they have the upper hand, so they use it to their benefit. This is a clear example of an insurance company that blatantly disregards the law and does whatever benefits them with no consequences.

FILING A LAWSUIT IN FEDERAL COURT

When an insurance company affirms its decision to terminate your ERISA claim, after an appeal, your attorney will file a lawsuit in federal court. This can be done in any state. No additional evidence is allowed to be submitted in the case, so if you forget a key piece of evidence, it is tough luck. This is why it is important to submit all relevant medical records when you are appealing your case. This is not a trial, there are no witnesses, and you will not testify. The judge will decide based on the evidence submitted.

Here is the even crazier part. Even if the judge believes you are disabled, they may not be able to reverse the decision, if the insurance company's process for arriving at their decision is "reasonable". If we win the case, the insurance company will pay us what is owed and, in some cases, our attorney fees. There are no penalties for them lying or terminating our policy despite strong evidence that we are still disabled, so there is nothing to disincentivize them. The entire process is stacked against us.

Appealing a decision can take up to one year, but several attorneys with whom I have spoken have said that it's highly possible the insurance company will try to settle before the case goes to trial.

Let's recap the length of time it could take to receive our long-term disability income if the judge decides in our favor. Once we are denied, we have ninety days to file an appeal. The insurance company then has a total of 90 days to respond, but as seen in my case, it took 113 days. The federal lawsuit could take up to one year. So, we are looking at about 18 months. For individuals like me who cannot return to work in any capacity, it is easy to see how bankruptcy could become a reality.

Private policies are governed by state laws, and we can sue for "bad faith", which would require the insurance companies to not just pay the policy benefits, but attorney fees and other damages such as compensation for financial loss, and emotional distress connected to those losses.

IMPORTANT CONSIDERATIONS AND MISTAKES TO AVOID

There are several different things that can happen when you're fighting for what's yours. As you do that, some of the most important factors that you need to consider include:

- **Budget/emergency fund:** Modify your budget to reflect what you have coming in and going out. The reality is that during this time, your emergency fund will become depleted. If you receive any lump sum cash, it will be a good resource to keep as a cushion.

- **Passive Income:** Now is the time to think about ways to generate passive income that can help supplement any other income that you are receiving. Even if you have an emergency fund, it may not be enough in the long term.

- **Understand your benefits**: If you have read your policy and still do not understand it, contact your human resource office to learn more about how your policy works, or invest in a long-term disability attorney and have them explain your benefits to you.

- **Get a supplemental policy**: Purchase a supplemental disability policy that you can customize to work for you. We have already described the many benefits of this in earlier chapters.

- **Do not miss deadlines:** Whenever I was given a deadline, I always did my best to respond right away, even if it was to say that I am unable to get this back to them by the deadline. I would provide my reasons and indicate when I could realistically get back to them. I always did my best to stay within the newly proposed deadline.

- **Review your doctor's records:** Do not allow an insurance company to use incorrect information in your records to deny or terminate your claim. Review everything that is being sent to them by your medical providers. That was a huge mistake that I made.

- **Optimism vs. Reality:** Do not be so optimistic about your healing journey that you neglect to do things you should do. For example, I neglected to follow up on my Social Security disability income application because I just never felt I would need it at all. This income will be a great supplement while you go through the appeals process for your ERISA policy. Although you ultimately may need to reimburse these amounts to the insurance company if you succeed in your appeal, it could be a great resource during this time. If you have children under eighteen, the income they receive can help with their expenses.

- **Be mindful of social media posts:** Insurance companies scrutinize everything. To avoid questions and extra scrutiny, watch what you post.

PHYSICAL SURVEILLANCE

As was mentioned in the previous chapter, insurers will hire a third-party investigator to follow you for days at a time while recording videos and taking photographs of you. The insurance company's goal is to "catch" you doing things inconsistent with your claim. It will use any damaging information it obtains as "proof" to deny your claim.

Although the insurance company can follow you at any time, my understanding is that there are certain times when it is more likely to conduct surveillance, such as around claim-related appointments, field interviews, or when meeting with an independent medical examination ("IME").

COPING WITH LOST BENEFITS WHILE GOING THROUGH THE APPEALS PROCESS

During the time that you are waiting for the appeals process, you still need to pay your monthly healthcare benefits and all your other expenses. Have a plan in place for how you will navigate your finances during this period?

I also want to add one more jolt of unpleasant reality. Your private disability insurance company can also terminate your policy and you would have to go through the same process. Both can happen during the same period.

Recall that I was evaluated by both companies at the same time. Thankfully, my private disability insurance company did the right thing after reviewing my records and maintained that I continue to meet the disability definition. The income they are providing along with my other resources have been very helpful in helping me manage my expenses. The reality, however, is that the loss of income from my ERISA policy and the reduction in my passive income due to the squatter living in my apartment rent free for over eighteen months has been extremely challenging financially.

I wish I could tell you that other things won't pop up; unfortunately, they will. Finding ways to preserve your mental health will be crucial. Use whatever resources that will help you through this period and continue to focus on your healing.

WORKING WITH A DISABILITY ATTORNEY

I realized very early on the risks of handling my disability termination on my own. When I learned that if I appeal my claim and submit my own records and my policy is still not reinstated, the courts will not allow any new records to be entered as evidence, I felt the benefit of an attorney outweighed the costs. There are several benefits to working with an attorney:

- **Expertise:** Lawyers have in-depth knowledge of the long-term disability system. They can analyze complex situations and develop effective strategies.

- **Experience:** The law firms have handled dozens of cases like yours before, probably with the same insurance company. They understand the legal precedents, common arguments, and potential pitfalls. This experience can be invaluable in achieving a favorable outcome.

- **Advocacy:** A lawyer acts as your advocate, representing your best interests throughout the legal process. They can negotiate on your behalf, gather evidence, and argue your case in court if necessary. I also believe that having an attorney may deter some activities of insurers.

While I am a big proponent of working with any attorney, I believe it is important to also share some of the drawbacks. These include:

- **Cost:** Legal fees can be expensive. Depending on the law firm, billing is either based on hourly rates or a flat fee. Make sure you understand the fee structure upfront and get everything in writing.

- **Time Commitment:** Legal matters can take time to resolve. There will be paperwork, meetings, and potentially court appearances. Be prepared to dedicate time to working with your lawyer throughout the process.

- **Emotional Toll:** Legal issues can be stressful. While a lawyer can help navigate the legal aspects, the emotional strain can be significant.

The journey to finding an attorney can be a stressful process on its own because you want to get it right, and you won't know if you got it exactly right until you begin going through the process. I did many consultations, only opting for the ones that were 100% free.

The first set of attorneys I contacted offered two options. One was a retainer of $30,000 upfront. That option was clearly out of the picture because I did not have that type of money! The second option was more appealing: I would not pay anything upfront. They would take a 25% cut of whatever they recovered for me.

For example, let us say I was receiving $10,000 a month in disability benefits and it took my attorneys three months to reinstate my policy. I would be entitled to $30,000 in total benefits. They would deduct $7,500 from that amount and send me a check for $22,500.

There was one additional clause, however, that was extremely troubling. I would be required to pay them 15% of any future disability income that I receive for as long as I remain on disability. In addition, if I wanted them to handle any further requests from the long-term disability company (e.g., requests for medical records), they would charge an extra 15% every month.

As an accountant and financial coach, I sat with the lawyer, knowing what my doctor had said about my uncertain recovery. I asked her, "So, if I remain disabled for another two years, this is how much I will owe you?" quoting the $84,500 that I will break down below. She confirmed my calculations with a "yes." I did not think that arrangement was in my best interest, and thought they were taking advantage of people in their worst moments, so I moved on.

Here is how it would play out: Let us say my disability benefits, which were terminated at the end of March, were reinstated in August and I was receiving $10,000 monthly.

- I would receive $50,000 from the insurance company for those five months and would need to pay the attorneys $12,500 (25%).

- If I remained on disability for another 24 months, I would receive $240,000, of which I would pay the attorneys and an additional $36,000 (15% of all future income).

- Then if I had retained them to continue to represent me during that period for any additional request by the insurance company, I would need to pay them an additional $36,000 (15%).

- In this scenario, for the total time that I receive disability benefits, I would pay them $84,500 out of the $290,000 that I received.

I went with a law firm that had a flat fee — 33% of the income that I received once the policy was reinstated. If the policy is not reinstated, I pay nothing. That means, if we use the same example above, I will pay this company $16,500. If I decided to use them for ongoing monitoring, I would pay an additional $36,000 but would still end up saving $32,000. Many of the other companies I spoke with had a similar payment arrangement as the firm that I chose. My visual friends, this table is for you.

	Attorney 1			Attorney 2	
	Income	Payment to Attorneys		Payment to Attorneys	
5 Months Income	$50,000	$12,500	{a}	$16,500	{a}
24 Months Future Income	240,000	36,000	{b}	0	
Ongoing Monitoring		36,000	{c}	36,000	{c}
Total	**$240,000**	**$84,000**		**$52,500**	
Difference		**$32,000**			

{a} Winning the appeal (25% Attorney 1 & 33% Attorney 2)
{b} 15% Payment on all future disability income
{c} 15% Representation fee for ongoing request from insurer

ARE ATTORNEYS WORKING IN YOUR BEST INTEREST?

Here is my personal point of view based on my experience. I do not believe a law firm that only gets paid if your case is successful will take on your case if they do not believe that you will win your appeal, because that is how they get paid. For the ones that charge a retainer, I would give them some credit that they too would not take your case if they did not believe they would be successful.

My concerns with those firms are two-fold, the large upfront cash outlay when you are trying to preserve your cash, and the risk that if you are not successful in your appeal, that money will not be recovered. When you choose an attorney that only collects if you win, there is no financial risk to you.

Here is the cynical side of me. I believe these firms want to ensure that they get the most that they can, so they drag your case out as long as they can.

What do I mean by that? Let's take both of my terminations. Both times, it took my attorneys almost 90 days to submit the appeals to the insurance company. I wanted the process to move along swiftly so that my income could be reinstated as soon as possible and frankly, my goal was to pay them as little as possible. I would therefore be proactive in following up with my attorneys to ascertain status, and volunteer to do whatever I needed to move the process along. Yet, they dragged their feet in getting the doctor's records and only included me in the process when they were bumping up on the deadline.

One might wonder what benefit they would gain from doing this. Well, if they wait for almost 90 days to submit the appeal, that guarantees them a minimum of 3 months of my income at the 33% fee, if they win the case. The insurer then has 45 days plus another 45-day extension. So, if the insurer takes the full 90 days, my attorneys will receive one-third of the six months of income that I was entitled to.

Compare that to them submitting the appeals memo within a month, and the insurance company taking two months to decide. They would then only be entitled to three months of the income that I received.

Even if my cynical unscientific theory is true, I will say this to you once again. Do not go it alone. The benefit of having an attorney far outweighs the cost. Here are some tips on **finding the right attorney:**

- **Area of Expertise:** Choose a lawyer who specializes in the specific legal area of your case. I would go with a firm that has experience in different states and, if possible, has filed appeals against that insurance company as well.

- **Experience:** Ask about the lawyer's experience with cases like yours and in your state.

- **Fees:** Get quotes from several lawyers and ensure that you understand their fee structure and work process before deciding.

- **Communication Style:** It is important to feel comfortable and be able to communicate effectively with your lawyer.

- **References:** Many of these law firms have testimonials online. You can review those or ask for references from past clients to get a sense of the lawyer's work ethic and results.

- **Ultimately, the decision to hire a lawyer is a personal one.** Consider the complexity of your situation, your resources, and your comfort level with the legal system.

You will find that some attorneys will charge a consultation fee, while for others it is complimentary. The decision about whether you want to pay for a consultation is up to you. Many of these firms that charge a consultation fee will put the fee towards your total cost if you retain them. For a more effective meeting, have a summary of your condition, your claim history, the denial letter, and your list of questions.

MANAGING THE ATTORNEY-CLIENT RELATIONSHIP

Some of the key things that you need to be aware of include:

- **Communication:** Keep your lawyer informed of any updates or developments in your case. Ask questions about anything that is unclear.

- **Be proactive:** Gather any relevant documents or information that might be helpful for your case.

- **Set realistic expectations:** Lawyers cannot guarantee outcomes. Discuss the potential risks and rewards of different approaches.

- **Fee Management:** Discuss what fees are included in your agreement and track your expenses.

Once you hire an attorney, all communication with the insurance company will go through them. If you decide to part ways with your attorney after winning the appeal, you'll need to complete paperwork to inform the insurance company of your decision.

MYTHS AND REALITIES OF DISABILITY INSURANCE

Myths	Realities
Completing all the required documents and providing medical evidence means that you will be treated fairly during the process.	Completing all the required documents and providing medical evidence means that you will be treated fairly during the process.
Being approved for social security benefits guarantees your continued receipt of long term disability benefits.	Insurance companies are not bound by social security decisions.
If your doctor or employer says you are disabled, then your long term disability company must pay your benefits.	LTD insurance companies has clause in their policies that effectively says that they have sole discretion to determine if you are disabled.
If the insurance company treats you unfairly you can file a lawsuit.	If you have an ERISA policy you must first go through the appeals process and only after that process is upheld, then you can file a lawsuit. You can only file a lawsuit if you have a private policy which is state regulated.
Your doctors and other providers will testify on your behalf at trial to help you win your case.	For ERISA policies, there are no trials. Neither you nor any medical providers will be present. The only evidence that will be used in the case is evidence submitted in the appeal process.

KEY TAKEAWAYS

- **Insurance Companies' Profit Motive:** Insurance companies prioritize profit, and every claim paid out affects their bottom line. So, expect scrutiny and resistance when filing claims or receiving disability income.

- **Understanding Denials**: Insurance companies may deny or terminate benefits if they believe your condition has improved or if there are discrepancies in your application. Be prepared to address these issues with your doctor and provide updated documentation if necessary.

- **Persistence Pays Off:** Don't back down if your claim is denied or discontinued. Insurance companies may employ tactics like delaying processes or outright lying. Stay vigilant and persist in advocating for your rights.

- **Seek Legal Assistance:** Consider hiring a long-term disability attorney to navigate the appeals process. Attorneys offer expertise, experience, and advocacy, increasing your chances of success and reducing stress.

- **Document Everything:** Keep meticulous records of medical evidence, communications with the insurance company, and any activities related to your disability claim. These records can strengthen your case during appeals.

- **Stay Informed:** Understand the appeals process and your rights as a policyholder. Be aware of deadlines and requirements for submitting appeals and seek assistance if needed.

- **Be Wary of Surveillance:** Insurance companies may conduct surveillance to gather evidence against your claim. Exercise caution on social media and be mindful of activities that could be misconstrued.

- **Cost/Benefit Analysis:** Understand the financial implications of hiring an attorney and weigh the costs against the potential benefits.

- **Choose Your Attorney Wisely:** When selecting a disability attorney, consider their expertise, experience, communication style, and fee structure. Ensure they align with your needs and goals for your case.

- **Understand the Myths & Realities:** There are many different types of misinformation floating around about LTD that you need to be aware of to make more informed decisions.

Winning your appeal for long-term disability benefits can be an uphill battle, but this chapter provided you with some great advice on how to fight for what you deserve. We talked about meeting deadlines, gathering strong evidence, and having a financial plan during the wait. I also mentioned getting a lawyer to keep you protected.

Now, let's shift gears to another potential lifeline beyond LTD—Social Security Benefits. It's crucial not to overlook this option. While the process is complex, I'll offer some general advice to help you get started with applying for Social Security Disability Income.

CHAPTER 7

Do Not Ignore SSDI: It Can Be A Lifeline

—Seize every opportunity to better your life, for the earliest action reaps the richest rewards."

You wake up each morning determined to face the day, but your disability throws up hurdles that make everyday tasks a struggle. Maybe it is chronic pain, limited mobility, or a cognitive impairment. Financial security shouldn't be another hurdle. Social Security benefits can be a crucial lifeline, offering financial help during challenging times. But what exactly are they?

WHAT ARE SOCIAL SECURITY BENEFITS?

Social Security benefits are income provided by the federal government to people at various stages of life. A component of this is SSDI, which is an income benefit provided to people with disabilities who are no longer able to work, their dependent children, and, in some instances, their spouse. These benefits can assist in maintaining a basic standard of living and easing the financial burden during a disabling event.

One of the benefits of SSDI is that it is not affected by how much money you have in the bank or whether you own property.

People often confuse SSDI with Supplemental Security Income (SSI), a needs-based program for elderly, blind, and disabled individuals with limited income. As a result, many people miss out on applying for this benefit.

To obtain Social Security disability benefits, an individual must generally prove that they are unable to engage in any substantial gainful activity that is expected to last for at least 12 continuous months or to result in death. Social Security looks at overall employability and skills in determining whether the medical condition stops you from working.

Now remember that we talked about the amount that you receive from SSDI typically reducing your income under your ERISA policy.

The question you might ask is: Why go through the hassle of applying for social security if it will reduce your income from your long-term disability policy? Well, there are several reasons such as:

1. Your long-term disability insurance company may require that you apply for this benefit and could discontinue paying you if you do not apply.

2. Your young children may receive benefits based on your disability. This additional income can help offset some of your children's expenses. For example, this benefit would help to offset my daughter's ongoing medical needs that are not covered by insurance.

3. You will have that income to help fill the gap if your long-term disability insurer terminates your income.

However, the SSDI safety net does have a few complexities. Here's what I'm talking about:

- While to collect social security retirement, a worker must have earned 40 credits over their working life, it becomes more complicated for SSDI, where the credit accumulation varies with the worker's age. For example, most people over 31 who seek to qualify must have earned at least 20 credits within the ten-year period prior to the onset of disability.

- Applicants must prove that they will be unable to work for a period of at least 12 months, unless the applicant has a condition so severe that it is included in Social Security's list of "compassionate allowances."

- Even assuming the applicant can meet the 12-month requirement, benefits cannot begin until month six because the program has a five-month waiting period, during which time no benefit is payable.

- If the application filing is delayed, benefits can only be awarded retroactively for up to a year.

- Initial applications are often denied, and it may take more than a year to receive benefits. The great news is that if you use the services of an attorney, there is a cap on the maximum amount of fees that they can charge you.

- SSI can fill this waiting period gap, but you must have little or no income and resources, have a disability or blindness, and be over the age of 65. On average, it can take up to six months to receive a response after applying.

SSDI has a *"trial work period"* of nine months. If you return to work and earn above a certain amount, those earnings are counted towards your trial period. You will not be penalized, as they view it as your attempt to return to work.

There is also an extended trial work period of 36 months. Like the nine-month period, it has a specific earnings limit. If your earnings stay below this limit during the 36 months, you will continue to receive benefits. However, if your earnings exceed that threshold in any month, your benefits for that month will stop. If you're still within the 36-month window, benefits can resume in following months if your earnings drop back below the threshold.

There is a cap on the amount that you can receive for SSDI, and it is likely to be inadequate as the sole source of income for a previously employed individual, especially if you are a high-income earner. Many people without employment tend to bridge the gap with personal savings, credit cards, home equity lines of credit, or loans from employer-sponsored retirement savings.

While I do not encourage withdrawals from retirement accounts, there are times when it may become necessary, but that should be one of your last resorts. It is important to note that withdrawals necessitated by the disability of the individual or a family member do not trigger an early withdrawal penalty, even if taken under age 59; however, you will be taxed.

Despite such temporary remedies, private disability insurance often stands as a strong restraining force that will prevent you from landing in an adverse situation and steering you too far off course financially.

WHEN CAN YOU APPLY?

Apply for SSDI as soon as you become eligible. If it turns out you are no longer disabled, you simply will not receive benefits, but at least you will have gone through the process. Besides, the process is so long and tedious that the earlier you start, the better.

Since I lived in denial for over a year and a half, while I applied early on, I never followed up and had to start the process all over again with the help of an attorney. I later discovered that the insurance company for my

ERISA policy had an organization that would work with me in applying. Neither my claims manager nor my return-to-work coordinator ever mentioned this information to me. I only learned about it when I was re-reading the initial packet that was sent to me.

By waiting so long to apply, I missed out on at least 18 months of benefits. This income could have helped during this period of going through the appeals process for my ERISA policy, and with my daughter's medical expenses, since she would have been receiving benefits.

PREPARING FOR YOUR INTERVIEW AND EXAMINATION

The SSA may schedule an interview with you for an independent medical examination. Here's how to be prepared:

Interview:

- **Gather medical records:** Obtain copies of your medical records from all doctors and specialists you see. Highlight sections that support your disability claim.

- **Bring your medication:** You will be asked about all the medications that you are taking. When setting up the appointment, they may ask you to take them with you.

- **Practice answering questions:** Anticipate questions about your limitations and daily activities. Prepare clear and concise answers that showcase the impact of your condition on your ability to work.

- **Be honest and consistent.** Don't exaggerate your limitations. Be truthful and consistent with the information you provide throughout the application process. Answer the question and don't overshare.

Examination:

- **Cooperate with the Doctor:** Follow the doctor's instructions during the examination. Answer any questions honestly.

- **Bring a Support Person:** Consider bringing a family member or friend who can corroborate your limitations.

- **Provide Additional Medical Evidence:** If you have additional medical evidence not already submitted, bring it to the examination.

- **Prepare to Spend Hours:** You may get lucky, and they go by your interview time, but don't be surprised if you must wait for many hours, especially if you have two IME on the same day.

MANAGING AND COORDINATING SOCIAL SECURITY BENEFITS

Imagine finally securing disability benefits—a significant victory. But the journey doesn't end there. You will come head-to-head with the task of managing and coordinating them with other potential income sources. I have a few tips that will come in handy:

- **Communication is key:** Always inform the SSA promptly about any changes in your income, living situation, or marital status.

This ensures you receive the correct benefit amount and avoids complications.

- **Potential Overlap:** Always disclose all income sources to the SSA to ensure accurate benefit calculations.

- **Explore additional resources**: Depending on your needs, explore programs like Medicaid or Medicare to supplement your disability benefits. These programs can help cover medical expenses not covered by traditional insurance.

POTENTIAL CHALLENGES AFTER APPROVAL

Your SSDI approval will come with some ongoing requirements. The Social Security Administration may perform a continuing disability review to assess your condition.

Complying with the Rules while receiving your benefits

- **Reporting Changes:** It is crucial to promptly report any changes, such as starting a part-time job, experiencing improvement in your medical condition, or a change in your address.

- **Appointment Attendance:** Always attend any scheduled medical examinations or consultation requests. These appointments are essential to maintaining your benefits.

Protect your rights for the long run

To protect your rights, you must first know them, so try as much as possible to familiarize yourself with the basic rules and regulations surrounding SSDI through the Social Security Administration website or by consulting with a disability advocate.

SHOULD YOU GET AN ATTORNEY FOR YOUR SSDI CLAIM?

Due to the complex nature of the process, I decided after filing for the first time on my own, to use an attorney when I applied the second time. Since there is a cap on how much an attorney can receive, I was willing to take the trade-off of paying those fees.

If you are trying to decide if you should involve an attorney or do it on your own, here are factors to consider:

- **Complexity of Your Case:** If your disability is straightforward and well-documented, you might be able to navigate the process on your own. But for complex cases involving multiple conditions, an attorney's expertise can be invaluable.

- **Financial Situation:** Hiring an attorney can be expensive, but they have the expertise, and they only get paid if you are approved.

- **Emotional Well-Being:** The SSDI application process can be stressful. An attorney can handle the legwork and address Social Security employees' requests, freeing you to focus on your health and well-being. You will still need to do some work, but they can let you know exactly what you need to do, instead of you having to try to figure it out.

- **Important Note**: Many organizations help with SSDI applications, including lawyer referrals. Be sure to consult with relevant professionals to ensure you get things done right.

SOCIAL SECURITY INCOME (SSI) VS SOCIAL SECURITY DISABILITY INSURANCE (SSDI) VS UNEMPLOYMENT

Most Americans are familiar with Social Security insurance; however, they are not fully clear on the different forms of social security income. I thought this brief overview might be helpful for those who want to understand it a bit better.

SSI, SSDI, and Unemployment benefits are all unique programs with different requirements for who can get them. You just might qualify for more than one, which means more benefits. Here is a quick overview of each:

- **SSI,** as briefly introduced earlier, is a program for individuals with low-income, little resources, aged 65 and up who are blind or disabled. Unlike SSDI, SSI has income and resource limitations rather than requiring a work history.

- **SSDI** replaces lost income for disabled workers with sufficient work history who meet the disability definition.

- **Unemployment benefits** are funded by state and federal taxes, and they provide short-term financial assistance to people who lose their jobs through no fault of their own while actively looking for new work. This program serves as a bridge for those who have lost their jobs until they can find new employment. While they all aim to provide financial assistance, these programs cater to distinct needs. Here's a breakdown to help you decide:

CAN YOU QUALIFY FOR MORE THAN ONE PROGRAM?

- In some situations, you might qualify for both SSDI and SSI. However, it is important to understand how they work together.

- It would not be advisable to apply for unemployment benefits while applying for or receiving long term disability. When you apply for unemployment, you are saying that you are willing and able to work, whereas applying for LTD indicates that you cannot work. These are contradictions, and decision makers can use them against you.

CHOOSING THE RIGHT PATH

Your work history and financial situation will influence whether you get SSDI or SSI benefits. If you've worked and paid into Social Security, SSDI provides a higher monthly benefit that is unaffected by your current income or assets. However, if you have limited income and resources, regardless of previous employment, and meet all the other requirements, SSI can help you meet your basic needs.

KEY TAKEAWAYS

- **SSDI** provides financial support to individuals with disabilities who are unable to work. You must have a sufficient work history and meet the Social Security Administration's definition of disability to qualify.

- **Applying for SSDI:** The application process can be lengthy and complex. It is recommended to apply as soon as you are eligible (even if you are unsure about approval) to avoid missing out on potential benefits.

- **Managing Benefits:** Once approved, you will need to manage your SSDI alongside other income sources. Communicate any changes in income, living situation, or marital status to the SSA promptly.

- **Interaction with LTD:** LTD insurance may offset your SSDI benefit. Carefully review your LTD policy to understand how this works.

- **Maintaining Benefits:** Maintaining eligibility requires complying with reporting changes in income, work activity, or health status. The SSA may also conduct reviews to verify your condition.

- **SSDI vs. Other Programs:** Understand the differences between SSDI, Supplemental SSI, and unemployment benefits. You may qualify for more than one program.

- **Protecting Your Rights:** Familiarize yourself with SSDI regulations and consider seeking legal assistance from a disability advocate or attorney, especially for complex cases.

If you are suffering from a disabling event and have not considered social security benefits as a financial resource, I encourage you to start the process right away. I thought I was well secured until life happened, and reality showed me I wasn't prepared. If I could go back in time, I would have applied for Social Security right away—you can't afford to leave loose ends that are critical to your finances.

It can feel like our lives, hopes, and dreams slowly die off when disability hits, but, in truth, it only dies if you let it. You can build a new life after a disabling event; the next chapter discusses just how.

CHAPTER 8

A New Day Has Dawned: **Plans to Transition Back into The Real World**

—Life's beauty lies in its new beginnings, far outnumbering the ugly ends."

Looking back to the period before I had the car accident, I was going through a transformation, but didn't even have a moment to stop and reflect. Oprah talks about life speaking to you in whispers, which many times is the first warning, and if you ignore it, sooner or later you will get a scream.

I believe my whisper came in the fall of 2020. I started working in my business in my last semester of graduate school in early 2020 — right before the Covid shutdown started. I was working many hours daily at my job and would spend all my free time before and after work putting together the framework for my business. I had huge goals and tight deadlines.

One day in September, I woke up and something was wrong. I couldn't get out of bed. I thought perhaps I had Covid, but it was not. My illness required me to take time off from work and many months of testing. Yet, had no conclusive diagnosis.

Nine months later, I had finally recovered. My calendar was jam-packed, and I was charging full speed ahead. Then in a flash, the accident changed everything. Was the universe trying to tell me something? Was that the scream that Oprah talks about? I have lately dubbed the accident my redirection.

A disability can be a turning point. Forcing us to confront how we define success. Societal norms often paint success with a broad brush: high-powered careers, financial security, and a certain lifestyle. But what happens when a disabling condition makes those goals incompatible with your reality? This is where the magic of redefining success comes in.

I am not a therapist, but these are some of the advice I have been given by my therapists, and some of the things that have worked for me over time and especially during this phase of my journey.

LETTING GO OF THE PAST

Letting go of your pre-disability perception of success might seem like losing a piece of yourself. It is natural to mourn the possibilities that appear out of grasp. But clinging to the past can be like clinging to a life raft in a storm; it keeps you afloat, but it prevents you from reaching the shore, where fresh opportunities and growth await.

So, how can we cross this emotional hurdle and muster the resolve to let go?

ACKNOWLEDGE YOUR EMOTIONS

Allow yourself to grieve. Do not suppress your feelings of sadness, anger, or frustration. Let's talk about the elephant in the room, because I feel hypocritical about dishing out this advice. I still have not fully accepted my "new reality". I continue to struggle physically and mentally, but I believe with all my whole heart, that with the right therapies, I will get back to normal activities. Some may think it's delusional. So clearly, I need to continue to process my emotions. This chapter is therefore for me, as much as it is for you.

This is really difficult work. Journaling, talking to a therapist, and joining a support group are all resources to help us process our emotions. I will not underestimate this part of the journey and the tremendous amount of work that is needed.

Write a 'goodbye' letter. This may seem unusual, but it may be an effective way to acknowledge the past and convey your emotions. Write a letter to your previous concept of success, thanking it for everything it has taught you, and then releasing it with love. Last year, when I returned from India, I did this exercise. It was freeing. That is when I officially paused my business and began focusing exclusively on myself, my family and friends.

I visited friends I had not seen in years, made more time for family, did some deep work in therapy, uncovering emotional trauma that I had patched a Band-Aid on and kept busy avoiding, spent time helping my daughter navigate her illness, and spent days coloring – I never realized how relaxing it could be. It felt weird at first, but as time went on, it became freeing. I watched myself morph into someone completely new. This emotional piece of the journey has probably been the hardest.

SHIFT YOUR PERSPECTIVE

- **Reframe your disability:** Rather than viewing your disability as a constraint, consider it a unique collection of experiences that will continue to shape who you are. It is hard and might take time, but consistent efforts will get you there eventually. You can start by identifying the strengths you have developed through your impairment.

- **Concentrate on what you can control:** You cannot change the past, but you can direct your attention and actions. Shift your focus from bemoaning missed opportunities to enjoying the thrilling possibilities of the present.

- **Find a silver lining:** Look for any unexpected benefits your disability may have provided. Perhaps it is a greater appreciation for the little things in life or a renewed connection to a supportive community.

EMBRACE THE POWER OF GRATITUDE

- **Practice daily gratitude:** Start a gratitude diary and jot down three things you are thankful for every day. Focusing on the good aspects of your life can help you change your mindset.

- **Celebrate your victories:** Recognize your achievements, no matter how modest. This could include learning a new skill, advocating for yourself, or simply having a pleasant day.

DISCOVERING NEW VALUES AND FINDING NEW POSSIBILITIES

This is a chance to reconnect with your core values. What truly matters to you? Is it creativity, connection, or personal growth? Maybe it is helping others or leaving a positive impact on the world. These values can guide you towards a new definition of success.

Experiment with new possibilities while keeping your values in mind. Perhaps a traditional career path is out of the question, but could you freelance or consult? Maybe your disability has opened doors to a new passion, like disability advocacy or art therapy. Consider the unique skills and strengths your disability has honed: resilience, problem-solving, or empathy.

One of my big goals now is to educate people about the importance of preparing for a disabling event. While I had always encouraged clients to purchase disability insurance, had I not gone through this experience, I would have never written this book, or given my TEDx talk. Living through this first-hand also gives me a deeper insight into how I can help others. I plan to continue to educate the masses about the importance of disability insurance, while pushing for changes in the disability law for ERISA policies.

EXPLORATION IS KEY

The beauty of this quest lies in its exploration. Think outside the box and embrace new activities you might never have considered before. Here are some ways to get started:

- **Reflect on what ignites you:** What sparks your curiosity? Is it a genre of music you've never listened to? Is there a historical period you find fascinating? Make a list of these interests, no matter how unconventional.

- **Consider accessibility:** Many activities can be adapted to fit your needs. Research online resources or talk to instructors about modifications that can make an activity accessible.

- **Volunteer your skills:** Giving back to your community can be incredibly rewarding. Look for volunteer opportunities that utilize your strengths and passions.

EMBRACE THE POWER OF CONNECTION

Remember, you don't have to go it alone. Finding a community of people who share your interests can be a huge source of motivation and support. Here are some ways to connect:

- **Join online communities:** Online forums and social media groups can connect you with people who share your passions, no matter your location.

- **Take a class:** Learning alongside others can be a great way to stay engaged and motivated. Many community centers and adult education programs offer a variety of classes for all abilities.

- **Find a mentor:** Look for someone who shares your interests and can offer guidance and encouragement.

GET A THERAPIST

Most of us think that we can go it alone; until we hit rock bottom. That drop can be hard and steep. Don't wait until you see yourself plummeting to reach out for help. Therapy was nothing new for me. I had gone on and off for many years, and always felt like I knew when it was time to check myself in.

This time, it took a while. Denial lingered with me for so long, and I believed every word it was telling me. By the time I started therapy, I was shattered in so many ways—but here's the silver lining. I was so vulnerable that issues I had avoided for decades just poured out of me.

I remember a 3-hour session with my therapist in which I didn't give her a moment to speak. I realized then how much baggage I was carrying and was ready to start letting go. So many of us are traveling through this life with unhealed wounds. Sometimes an unexpected, disabling event is our wake-up call.

THE IMPORTANCE OF STAYING ENGAGED

Staying engaged in activities you enjoy has a profound impact on your well-being. It can reduce stress, boost self-confidence, and foster a sense of purpose. Even small moments of joy can make a big difference.

SUCCESS REDEFINED

Redefining success does not mean replacing one big achievement with another. It is about creating a rich tapestry of experiences and accomplishments that reflect your current situation and basic values. Success is redefined as a dynamic journey rather than a fixed destination.

SUCCESS IS MULTIFACETED

- **Mastery in the Face of Adversity:** Learning a new skill to help you adapt to your impairment is a victory. It showcases your tenacity, resourcefulness, and unyielding spirit. Celebrate these important milestones, both big and small!

- **The Power of Connection:** Establishing a strong support network is an effective form of self-care. Surround yourself with individuals who will inspire, support, and celebrate your unique journey. This network becomes a source of strength and a platform for future expansion.

- **Finding joy in the ordinary:** Sometimes success is as simple as recognizing the beauty that surrounds us. It could be the sun's warmth on your face, laughter with a loved one, or the calm satisfaction of completing a chore. Learning to cherish these times promotes contentment and tranquility.

EMBRACE THE UNIQUENESS OF YOUR PATH

Success isn't one-size-fits-all. What brings fulfillment to one person might not resonate with another. Your journey is shaped by your own experiences, values, and dreams. Focus on what ignites your passion and gives your life meaning and purpose.

LIVING AUTHENTICALLY

Success is about living truthfully in accordance with your principles. What really matters to you? Is it about being creative, connecting, and making a difference in the world? Align your objectives and activities with these ideals. When you live with integrity and purpose, you will experience a sense of fulfillment that goes beyond external measurements of accomplishment. Some of the things worth remembering to include:

- You are not defined by your disability.

- There is no one-size-fits-all definition of success.

- Celebrate your progress, big and small.

- Focus on what brings you joy and meaning.

Redefining success is an ongoing process. As your life evolves, so too will your definition. Embrace the journey, and you will find success that is truly yours.

ADVOCATING FOR CHANGE: MY EXPERIENCE IN THE INSURANCE INDUSTRY

For eleven years, I worked in the insurance industry, witnessing firsthand the significant resources dedicated to lobbying efforts. Only the pharmaceutical industry outpaces insurance companies in lobbying expenditures. These vast annual sums translate into real power to shape regulations that favor the industry.

The Case of ERISA

The regulations surrounding ERISA serve as a prime illustration of how lobbying dollars can heavily influence policies in favor of insurance companies. Consumers, unfortunately, bear the brunt of these negative consequences.

Needed Reforms for ERISA Transparency

ERISA regulations are ripe for reform, particularly regarding transparency in insurer practices. While some amendments represent a step in the right direction, significant improvements are necessary. Here are some key changes that need to be made:

1. **Trial Work Period:** Social Security has a trial work period where individuals can attempt to return to work over a certain period, without losing their benefits. There should be rules in place that require insurance companies to provide a similar benefit, so that workers can assess whether they are able to work in their own occupation or another occupation, and not immediately lose their benefits. They should never be kicked off their benefits without first being given an opportunity to find a job.

2. **Grace Period:** Employees should have the opportunity to resume their disability benefits if they have attempted to work for a certain period and it is not feasible due to their existing medical condition.

3. **Penalties for disregarding deadlines:** Insurance companies should face strict penalties for disregarding the deadline for deciding on an appeal. The claimant should automatically be granted the full amount of their benefits when such an event occurs.

4. **Penalties for acting in bad faith:** Insurance regulators, the federal government, and employers should enforce strict penalties on insurers when they are found to have lied to support denying or terminating a case.

HOLDING EMPLOYERS ACCOUNTABLE

Apart from a few states, employers are not legally required to offer disability insurance to their employees. It is a sweetener to their benefits package. While healthcare benefits may be a bigger factor in driving decisions about whether to take a job with an employer, long term disability may not be a big driver.

We generally just accept that we have it and believe that if we become disabled, we will be covered. Most of us do not know the details of this benefit and, sadly, most of us only discover what we have and how it works when it is too late to do anything about it.

I would like to see more employers take a proactive approach to educating their employees about this benefit. I think it is also important that these employers evaluate the long-term disability company they are selecting to provide these benefits. If an employer truly values the well-being of its employees and wants to offer benefits that can be valuable to them if they become disabled, this should be reflected in the terms of the policy contract with the insurance company as well as the reputation of the insurer that is administering their long-term disability policy.

I believe that if employees become more educated about their policies and their long-term disability carrier, they will begin to hold their employers more accountable to provide better benefits that will sustain them during their time of disability.

LIVING A FULFILLING LIFE

I went from being the queen of multitasking to not being able to do simple tasks. Everything became an overwhelming task. Tasks that I could complete in an hour would now take a day or longer. The daily chronic pain I experienced, coupled with daily migraines for six months, really took its toll on me and resulted in a deterioration of my mental capacity.

After a trip to Bali for my birthday, where I found peace for 10 beautiful days, I realized I needed to take a step back, but was too stubborn to make such a drastic move. A month later, I flew to India with my daughter, who was also going through a crippling battle with multiple medical issues. We found not just peace but healing through Ayurvedic medicine.

The unbearable pain from the botched steroid shots, and other symptoms from the accident were significantly reduced. Those 16 days in treatment gave me so much time for thinking and reflection. I accepted that life was no longer the same and although I stopped short of believing that I could not go back to what it used to be, I made many changes.

You will decide what fulfillment means to you. What you will stop or do more of. How you will practice self-care and maintain a positive outlook, and ultimately how you will navigate your disabling event with strength and determination.

KEY TAKEAWAYS

Letting Go of the Past:

- Acknowledge your emotions: Allow yourself to grieve lost possibilities. Techniques like journaling or joining support groups can help.

- Shift your perspective: See your disability as a unique set of experiences and focus on the strengths it has built.

- Embrace gratitude: Practice daily gratitude and celebrate your victories, no matter how small.

Discovering New Values and Finding New Possibilities:

- Reconnect with your core values: What truly matters to you? Use these to guide your new definition of success.

- Explore new possibilities: Consider alternative career paths, hobbies, or activities that align with your values and adapt to your needs.

Exploration is key:

- Reflect on your interests: What sparks your curiosity? Explore unconventional options and find accessible ways to pursue them.

- Volunteer your skills: Giving back can be rewarding. Look for opportunities that utilize your strengths and passions.

- Embrace the Power of Connection: Find a community of like-minded people for support and motivation. Online forums, classes, or mentorship can help.

The Importance of Staying Engaged:

- Stay engaged in activities you enjoy: It boosts well-being, reduces stress, and fosters purpose.

Success Redefined:

- Success is a journey, not a destination; it is a tapestry of experiences that reflects your values and current situation.

- Celebrate your progress: Recognize milestones, big or small, and find joy in the ordinary.

- Embrace the uniqueness of your path: There's no one-size-fits-all definition. Focus on what brings you fulfillment.

- Live authentically: align your goals and actions with your core values to achieve true fulfillment.

It is not a fresh start, but a fresh perspective and set of values that will help you build a life that you will be proud of. It is important that you keep your mind afloat and away from the thoughts that will keep you trapped in sadness, poverty, anxiety and depression. You will be building on everything you already have to make sure that you are indeed moving forward.

CONCLUSION

Empowering Your Financial Future **with Confidence**

—Your journey to financial security begins with understanding and preparation. Embrace the challenges, seek support, and take control of your future—one step at a time."

We've been talking about finances and disability, and it can feel like a lot to take in! But the good news is that by understanding the seven strategies to surviving and thriving if you become unexpectedly disabled, you can feel much more secure that you have a solid foundation on which to stand.

So, whether you're living with a disability now or just planning ahead, having this knowledge is like having a superhero toolkit for your finances. Let's recap each strategy.

CREATING A BUDGET AND EMERGENCY FUND

The foundation of financial security starts with a solid budget and an emergency fund. Budgeting allows you to manage your income and expenses effectively, ensuring you have a clear picture of your financial health.

An emergency fund is like having a safety net—it helps you handle unexpected expenses without going into debt. While it might mean making some adjustments to cover everything, in the long term, it's worth it.

UNDERSTAND LONG-TERM AND SHORT-TERM DISABILITY INSURANCE

Understanding the nuances of short-term and long-term disability insurance is crucial. These policies protect your income if you are unable to work due to a disability. Knowing the differences and ensuring you have adequate coverage helps safeguard your financial future, giving you peace of mind in the face of uncertainty.

GET THE RIGHT POLICY

Shopping for the right disability policy requires careful consideration and research. It's important to compare different options, understand the terms, and choose a policy that fits your specific needs. This section has provided you with the tools to make informed decisions that will allow you to select the best possible coverage.

SECURING AND KEEPING YOUR BENEFITS

Once you've got your policy, knowing how to secure and keep your benefits is key. That means understanding how claims work, sticking to deadlines, and keeping good records. Being informed and staying on top of things ensures you get the benefits you're entitled to.

FIGHT FOR YOUR BENEFITS AND KNOW PITFALLS TO AVOID

Sometimes you may need to fight for your benefits. This can involve appealing denied claims and navigating bureaucratic hurdles. Knowing common pitfalls and how to avoid them can make a significant difference in your ability to secure the support you need.

UNDERSTAND HOW TO NAVIGATE SSDI

Social Security Disability Insurance is another vital resource for those unable to work due to disability. Understanding how to apply for SSDI, what to expect during the process, and how to maximize your chances of approval is critical. This section demystified SSDI, providing clear guidance on navigating this federal program.

REBUILD AFTER DISABILITY WITH CONFIDENCE

Transitioning back to the real world after a disabling event can be challenging, but having a plan in place can ease this process. This includes setting new goals, seeking new opportunities, and leveraging support systems. Rebuilding your life after disability is a journey that requires a strategic approach, patience, and resilience.

CLOSING THOUGHTS AND A CALL TO ACTION

We can never be fully prepared for an unexpected life altering event, but by now, you have an arsenal of tools that will not only help you to lay the foundation, but also to utilize if you are one of those unfortunate one-in-four adults who do become disabled.

These strategies will help stave off the dreaded financial consequences and can save you from going into bankruptcy.

Just like having a fire extinguisher doesn't mean you expect a fire, being prepared for unexpected challenges by having enough long-term disability insurance and leveraging other financial strategies is invaluable and offers peace of mind. These strategies can help you cultivate strong support networks, navigate financial hurdles, and develop a positive outlook, all of which can benefit anyone on life's unpredictable journey.

Take the strategies in this book, implement the ones that you can now, and get a general understanding of the others. Supplement what you are doing in this book with the strategies that I have outlined in my book "Broke to Wealth" to build your financial fortress.

We all deserve to live a life that is fulfilling regardless of whether we are healthy or find ourselves with a disabling condition. We will need to put some work in to secure a solid foundation. But once we have built those foundations, having the knowledge will help us to adjust more quickly when life begins to throw us different curveballs.

Remember, you're not alone in this journey. With the right tools and support, you can navigate the challenges of disability with confidence and resilience. Take charge of your financial future today, and pave the way for a secure and fulfilling life, even if you do suffer a disabling event.

If you are seeking a community where you can learn and grow financially, join my community at growyourwealth10x.com to take your financial literacy knowledge even deeper. This is your chance to build a legacy that extends far beyond panic and fear of not being able to cope financially if you suffer a disabling event. Embark on a wealth-building journey with excitement and watch your dreams become reality!

Let's Start Today!

ABOUT THE AUTHOR

Tanya Taylor, CPA, MBA, is an award-winning author, speaker, and seasoned financial coach with over two decades of experience in teaching personal finance. Her dedication to empowering individuals to overcome financial barriers was born out of her desire to stop the cycle of poverty. Her compelling story, from being an impoverished Jamaican undocumented immigrant who traversed to the U.S. alone at 16 with $100, to building a million-dollar retirement before 48 and saving for her children's college, while traveling to over 60 countries, has inspired thousands worldwide.

Featured in prestigious publications such as Black Enterprise and Business Insider, she is known for her transformative insights on wealth building and financial literacy. Through her impactful speeches, coaching program, and media appearances, Taylor continues to lead a movement toward financial empowerment, guiding individuals to achieve financial freedom and security, regardless of their starting point.

HOW TO REACH ME

Website: Growyourwealth10x.com

LinkedIn: Tanya Taylor, CPA, MBA

Instagram: @growyourwealth10x.com

TikTok: @tanyataylorcpa

Email: Tanya@growyourwealth10x.com

Facebook: Tanya Taylor, CPA, MBA - Grow Your Wealth Community

NOTES